In today's society, with... high and dysfunction taking the place of normal behavior, the ministry of deliverance has never been more relevant or needed in the history of mankind. The church today, with all of its platitudes, props, and prosperity, needs to return to the power that shook the world, set the captive free, and changed the direction of mankind. This book by Iris and John Delgado to release the authority to destroy the works of the enemy is needed, necessary, and timely for this generation.

—MAURY DAVIS
SENIOR PASTOR, CORNERSTONE CHURCH
MADISON, TN

Dr. John Delgado and Dr. Iris Delgado, both anointed authors, have combined their anointing to share how every believer can break the power and influence of our enemy. Today, more than ever, people are struggling under spiritual attacks but are at a loss in how to deal with these issues in a proper and balanced approach. John and Iris walk in what they write. They see these principles work in their life as well as in the life of others. This book is a must-read, for it will enable you to rise up and walk in a new level of freedom in every area of your life.

—DR. NAOMI DOWDY
APOSTLE-EQUIPPER
NAOMI DOWDY MENTORING AND CONSULTING
FORMER SENIOR PASTOR, TRINITY CHRISTIAN
CENTRE, SINGAPORE

DESTROY
THE WORKS
OF THE ENEMY

DESTROY
THE WORKS
OF THE ENEMY

IRIS & JOHN
DELGADO

CHARISMA
HOUSE

Most CHARISMA HOUSE BOOK GROUP products are available at special quantity discounts for bulk purchase for sales promotions, premiums, fund-raising, and educational needs. For details, write Charisma House Book Group, 600 Rinehart Road, Lake Mary, Florida 32746, or telephone (407) 333–0600.

DESTROY THE WORKS OF THE ENEMY by Iris and John
   Delgado
Published by Charisma House
Charisma Media/Charisma House Book Group
600 Rinehart Road
Lake Mary, Florida 32746
www.charismahouse.com

Cover design by Justin Evans
Design Director: Bill Johnson

Visit the authors' website at www.crownedwithpurpose .com. You can also follow Iris on Facebook at Crowned with Purpose (Dr. Iris Delgado) or e-mail her at driris@ crownedwithpurpose.com.

Library of Congress Cataloging–in–Publication Data

Delgado, Iris.
  Destroy the works of the enemy / Iris and John Delgado. -- First edition.
    pages cm
  ISBN 978-1-62136-514-3 (trade paper) -- ISBN 978-1-62136-515-0 (ebook)
  1. Spiritual warfare--Biblical teaching. I. Title.
  BS680.S73D45 2013
  235'.4--dc23
                                        2013016305

While the author has made every effort to provide accurate telephone numbers and Internet addresses at the time of publication, neither the publisher nor the author assumes any responsibility for errors or for changes that occur after publication.

First edition

13 14 15 16 17 — 987654321
Printed in the United States of America

We dedicate this manual to all the people who minister deliverance and also to all the people who anxiously desire to be set free from the strongholds of the enemy. Many thanks to God's dedicated men and women who tenaciously stand in the gap, without fear of using the authority that Christ Jesus has delegated to all believers to set the captives free from spiritual prisons.

The deliverance ministry is not for everyone, but yes, everyone could be set free from the power of the enemy.

—*Iris and John Delgado*

Contents

INTRODUCTION

THIS HOW-TO FREEDOM manual will teach you how to use your authority in Christ Jesus. It is not meant to be an exhaustive textbook that takes an in-depth look at everything related to the enemy. Rather it is a compendium that covers much of what you will need to know to walk in freedom from the attacks of Satan. It is our desire that this book will teach you how to understand your authority in Christ and how to use God's power to free your life from Satan's control. It will also inspire you to begin your own deeper study of God's Word to more thoroughly understand the strategies of the enemy and to learn to apply God's power to every area of bondage or confusion you may have experienced from the enemy. It will also help you to teach others to walk in the freedom and power of God.

The church today needs the ministry of setting people free from all kinds of bondage. Salvation is the first step. Deliverance from the effects of iniquities should be the second step.

We are entering a season of greater crisis and evil. The devil knows that he has a short time left, and he's tenaciously discouraging Christians who are not standing firm in Christ Jesus. A generation of Christians with lukewarm hearts is desperately looking for help from the alarming wave of diabolical attacks against them and their families.

The power of the Holy Spirit is one of the greatest inheritances of the kingdom of God. However, many Christians are not walking in the fullness of the power of the Holy Spirit. Demonic forces are at work in many lives, filling them with oppression and depression.

The world needs help. The church needs the ministry of setting the captives free from spiritual prisons. As believers we have authority over all the power of the enemy (Luke 10:19). But what are we doing with this power?

This book will also address the following subjects:

- Can a Christian have evil spirits?

- Our authority to overcome

- How to deal with fear

- How to be released from bondage

- How to recognize habits and practices that attract evil spirits

- How to put on the armor of God

- Does a believer have authority over sin and Satan?

- How to recognize true and false doctrines

- How to keep your freedom and live free

- Powerful declarations that counteract the attacks of the enemy

- Do evil spirits cause all of our problems?

Too many of God's people are almost totally ignorant of the nature of evil spirits and are fearful of things beyond man's natural understanding. Many choose to ignore this portion of God's ministry because they have not been taught the importance of their authority over all the power of the enemy. As a result, multitudes of precious believers are living in needless torment today, not able to enjoy victories in their lives.

God's people can live free from mental torment, fear, trauma from abuse, jealousy, hatred, lust, pride, self-pity, addiction, gluttony, and all other forms of bondage, oppression, and defilement.

There are two main causes of man's inner problems: The first is the *flesh* or the *old man*. This is man's carnal unregenerate, rebellious nature, which is influenced and buffeted by Satan. The second cause of the inner problems is *evil spirits,* which Satan uses to enslave some aspect of the *flesh,* and they will not relinquish their hold unless compelled to do so.

In many instances the church has occupied a rather passive role and a defeated attitude in the face of the enemy that rules in the world. God is saying to His church, "Rise up and rule in the midst of your enemies."

In all churches and ministries we can find believers who are being attacked by spirits of oppression and depression. Too many ministers are more than willing to leave the devil alone rather than try to deal with the spirits that torment people. But the time will come when they will have to deal with the tormenting spirits if they really want to see people set free from oppression. Knowledge about this subject is very vital.

The Bible references in this manual will increase your faith and reveal who we are in Christ Jesus and how we can become everything that Father God created us to be. Please read and meditate over each chapter carefully. Ask the Holy Spirit to illuminate the teaching to your spirit and seal it in your heart so that the enemy will not be able to steal the word of truth.

The Lord greatly bless you as you begin this journey toward freedom in Christ Jesus. May you receive the confidence and courage to share these truths with others who may be enslaved.

> Therefore if the Son makes you free, you shall be free indeed.
>
> —JOHN 8:36

The Kingdom of Heaven and Its Privileges

*Thy kingdom come. Thy will be done
in earth, as it is in heaven.*
—Matthew 6:10, KJV

I REMEMBER THE FEELING of euphoria and suspense I (Iris) had as an eight-year-old girl as I listened to my Sunday school teacher describe a story about the magnificence and beauty of life in heaven. I thought in my mind, "What must I do to get there?" But I don't remember hearing a story about what I could do in the meantime to enjoy the kingdom privileges here on earth. When she told us the story about hell, I remember being afraid for an entire week. When I got older and had a deeper understanding of the kingdom of God, its privileges, the kingdom of darkness, and a believer's authority over the enemy, I was even more amazed at realizing that so many people refuse to understand this subject. They are afraid of it, or they simply have never been taught the truth.

Few Christians have grasped the full meaning of what Jesus offered to the world when He proclaimed in Matthew 3:2, "Repent, for the kingdom of heaven is at hand!"

This teaching is very informative and necessary, and it is intended to inspire your mind to understand the importance of exercising your authority as a believer. We also desire that you understand the constant struggle we face between the kingdom of light and the kingdom of darkness.

THE KINGDOM OF GOD BEGINS ON EARTH

Some think of the kingdom as a beautiful land we inherit only after death. But to Jesus, this was not a place that man had to die to enter. The kingdom begins right here on earth and continues throughout eternity in heaven. Anyone who chooses to enter without reservations may become a citizen of the kingdom.

John the Baptist proclaimed the coming of the kingdom (Matt. 3:1–2). Jesus continued to preach the kingdom throughout His ministry. When He sent the twelve disciples out two by two, He commanded them to also preach about the kingdom (Luke 10:8–9).

Most of Jesus's preaching and teaching was about the kingdom, and many of His parables were meant to describe it. It was His most important message then, and so it is today. It was the most wonderful news to be heard on earth in the New Testament times, and it still is today.

How Can We Become a Citizen of the Kingdom?

If we choose to live in this kingdom, we must accept its King, its laws, and its responsibilities. With this comes perfect peace, because it sets us free from every letter and rule of the law. It sets us free from the bondage of sin, from sorrow and pain, and makes us fellow citizens with Jesus in the kingdom of heaven, whose King is Jesus, whose law is love, whose flag is the cross, and whose provider is God.

How can we become a part of this marvelous place? We must have a total allegiance to God above every man, organization, or country on earth. We must make a commitment to obey God rather than man.

> If anyone desires to come after Me, let him deny himself, and take up his cross, and follow Me. For whoever desires to save his life will lose it, but whoever loses his life for My sake will find it. For what profit is it to a man if he gains the whole world, and loses his own soul? Or what will a man give in exchange for his soul?
> —Matthew 16:24–26

First, we must be born again and committed to God to be partakers of God's kingdom. The kingdom of heaven and its wonderful privileges are not recognized or understood by all Christians. We have limited God and

3

His kingdom by our own limited thinking. We give our allegiance to small mundane passing things, and in so doing we miss the joy and wonders of this great kingdom, beginning right here on earth.

Our allegiance, in most cases, is to our family, business, denomination, or nation, each one confining us to a small role instead of God's vast plan for our lives. Jesus came and offered us a way of life so great and marvelous that we have not dared to drop our little gains and loyalties to be able to comprehend it.

PRIVILEGES OF THE KINGDOM OF GOD

1. It renews the unregenerate mind.

   And do not be conformed to this world, but be transformed by the renewing of your mind, that you may prove what is that good and acceptable and perfect will of God.
   —ROMANS 12:2

2. It frees the Christian from racial prejudice and superiority, because Jesus is King over all the earth and over every man and woman.

3. It delivers the Christian from the madness of wars, for he cannot fight or kill his brothers in Christ.

4. It eliminates the concern about our personal needs, because God promises to meet all of our needs if we first seek the kingdom of God and His righteousness.

Therefore do not worry, saying, "What shall we eat?" or "What shall we drink?" or "What shall we wear?" For after all these things the Gentiles seek. For your heavenly Father knows that you need all these things. But seek first the kingdom of God and His righteousness, and all these things shall be added to you.

—MATTHEW 6:31–33

5. It frees the Christian from covetousness, for in the kingdom no one owns anything. The believer and all his possessions belong to God.

6. It frees the Christian from worldliness.

For what profit is it to a man if he gains the whole world, and is himself destroyed or lost?

—LUKE 9:25

WHY IS THERE SO MUCH IGNORANCE ABOUT THE KINGDOM OF GOD?

Why do so many Christians cling to their little personal loyalties, which bring business against business, church against church, nation against nation, and man against God? It is because the principles and the blessings of the kingdom have not been taught to new believers. Many leaders frown on teaching such openhearted loyalty to God. It threatens their hold on their members. Governments have also tried to stamp out this worldwide loyalty to God, and for decades they have been very successful in suppressing Christianity.

As long as we reject or remain ignorant about the kingdom of God with its absolute allegiance to God, we will continue to search without success for a way to live in peace and happiness.

To enter into the kingdom, we must believe and accept four great truths:

1. That Jesus is the Son of God (John 20:31)

2. The death of Jesus and the everlasting atonement for all our sins (Heb. 2:17)

3. The resurrection of Jesus Christ (1 Pet. 1:3)

4. The great truth that Jesus sent another Helper, the Holy Spirit, on the Day of Pentecost (John 14:26; Acts 2:4)

We must believe not only that these great things really happened but also that they happened for our benefit.

We must accept these truths as a gift of God's love. We must be willing to identify ourselves with each of these events so that we may be born again and become sons and daughters of God. As sons and daughters of God, we are to walk in the steps of Jesus and follow the example of His holy, loving, and serving life.

How Can We Accomplish This New Freedom?

We can only walk in freedom with the help and the power of the Holy Spirit.

> The average Christian without the Holy Spirit cannot see, understand, or appreciate the greatness of the kingdom of heaven.

Neither can he perceive other believers from different denominations and many nations as one in Christ. Without the Holy Spirit the Christian cannot love his enemies or turn the other cheek.

To really enjoy our experience as children of God, we must truly be born again and transformed by the renewing of our minds. Then, and only then, does the kingdom of heaven seem possible or desirable to us. Only then will we be able to understand that in God's eyes the kingdom is more important than the United States or any other country. We will understand that doing good "unto the least of these" is more important than our racial pride and prestige and that the commandment "Thou shall not kill" is more important than national pride or military supremacy.

THE HOLY SPIRIT AS THE HELPER

The power of the Holy Spirit working in the believer is one of the greatest inheritances of the kingdom of God. It makes heaven both real and glorious. It provides divine direction to live victoriously here on earth.

If you have the Holy Spirit in your life, don't keep the power locked in! Allow God's Spirit to operate freely in your life so that you can be an effective overcomer in the kingdom of God here on earth.

If you do not have this precious gift of the Holy Spirit in your life as a believer, I recommend that you make a decision to accept this precious gift. *Being filled with the power of the Holy Spirit is the core and heart of the victory of a believer.*

> Then Peter said to them, "Repent, and let every one of you be baptized in the name of Jesus Christ for the remission of sins; and you shall receive the gift of the Holy Spirit. For the promise is to you and to your children, and to all who are afar off, as many as the Lord our God will call."
> —ACTS 2:38–39

PRAYER TO RECEIVE THE HOLY SPIRIT

Dear heavenly Father, I draw near to You with thanksgiving in my heart for the gift of salvation. Thank You for the desire that is in me for the living water of Your Word. I rejoice greatly for the understanding I am receiving of the importance of Your presence and Your Spirit dwelling in me. Thank You for the awareness that the fruit of the Spirit must be present in my life to live victoriously.

I now desire to be baptized in the name of Jesus Christ for the forgiveness of my sins, and I accept Your precious gift of the Holy Spirit. I now rejoice in this unity with Your Spirit that enables me to understand the things of the Spirit of God. Help me to never quench the Holy Spirit and to be quick to confess my sins.

Holy Spirit, grant me the honor and the freedom of praying in the Spirit. I receive this precious gift and will be careful to always give You all the glory and the honor You deserve. In the name of the Lord Jesus Christ, amen.

The Promise of Authority and Power of the Believer

THE SECRET OF WALKING IN AUTHORITY

You are of God, little children, and have over-
come them, because He who is in you is
greater than he who is in the world.
—1 John 4:4

UTHORITY IS POWER. It is the ability to have
influence over someone or something. It is consent to wield a command. It is assurance to direct
and implement. The Greek word for "power" is *exousia*,
which means "authority." Once you receive salvation
and have been delivered from the kingdom of darkness
to the kingdom of God, Satan no longer has *authority*
over your life. Now you have authority over Satan and
his demons. You don't have to work to earn this right. It
becomes your right in the name of Jesus. You really don't
have to claim it or beg for it. Whether you pray for it or
believe it or not, a believer has authority over sin and
over all the power of the enemy.

We must know and remember that this authority we have
is to always bring glory to God and not to ourselves.

Father God has given us the promise that He will back
us up every time we have the courage to step out in His
authority and use the power He's given to us over all the
power of the enemy. As a believer, once you step out in
faith and release the Word of God over a situation, you
will begin to see and partake of the promise and the
privilege of a being a joint heir with Christ Jesus.

It is true that some people have more authority than
others because they recognize the gift and operate in it
without fear. It is also true that if you know that you have
authority over the enemy but keep giving him an open
door to enter, he will definitely enter and exert his will
over your will.

THE BELIEVER'S AUTHORITY OVER SIN AND SATAN

Scripture is very specific. A born-again believer has
authority over sin and authority over Satan. Jesus gave
that authority when He said, "Behold, I give you the
authority to trample on serpents and scorpions, and over
all the power of the enemy, and nothing shall by any
means hurt you" (Luke 10:19). Paul expanded our understanding of our authority by teaching: "For sin shall not
have dominion over you, for you are not under law but
under grace" (Rom. 6:14).

We don't have to fall into the trap of believing

everything we hear and see going on in the world. The Holy Spirit gives us wisdom to recognize what is deception and what is truth. To overcome the world doesn't mean that we won't have problems and tribulations. But in the midst of the challenges and adverse circumstances we can have victory in Christ.

> For whatever is born of God overcomes the world. And this is the victory that has overcome the world—our faith.
>
> —1 JOHN 5:4

There are different degrees of authority that are determined by the degree of personal victory in a Christian's life. You must develop knowledge and discernment to understand the direction of the Holy Spirit and how you can use your authority in every situation.

The authority of Christ as a conqueror over evil spirits is not inborn in the believer. Through the power of the Holy Spirit, in response to faith, the believer is able to operate under this authority. In other words, you must overcome the evil forces that come against you by faith in the power of the name of Jesus. The Word of God doesn't say that we must be spiritually mature to exercise our authority but that we must be born again and believe in the Son of God.

> You are of God, little children, and have over-
> come them, because He who is in you is greater
> than he who is in the world.
>
> —1 John 4:4

Our faith extends God's authority to every area of our lives.

The secret of walking in authority and seeing results is very clear in John 8:31–32: "If you abide in My word, you are My disciples indeed. And you shall know the truth, and the truth shall make you free."

Many Christians can't perceive themselves using their authority to overcome the attacks of the enemy because of fear and doubt. You see, it's not that Satan is all-powerful and uses his authority to exert fear and torment in God's people, but the truth is that many believers are afraid of Satan and anything that has to do with evil spirits. Ignorance about this subject will keep a person away from anything that has to do with power and authority against evil. That is why discipleship about this topic is extremely important and necessary for every believer.

Please don't feel like we're condemning anyone. Our desire is to bring knowledge and truth, for we know that the truth will set people free.

The Importance of Commitment

Most people are achievers, striving to achieve goals, fame, prestige, fortunes, and so forth. But achievements are not what God is looking for in your walk with Him. He looks at your faith. How do you *overcome* in your life? How many spirits of the flesh have you conquered? Did you go all the way back to the cross and crucify the flesh with Jesus?

Can you humbly stand in God's presence completely stripped of all your fleshly desires, totally submitted to Him to be used as He sees fit? This is called *total commitment* and cannot be accomplished when there is any demonic activity in your life. When people are free from all entanglements from Satan, then total commitment becomes a way of life. It is then that you become an active overcomer and begin to possess your inheritance and freedom from the control of Satan. Then you begin to live victoriously under the faith covenant. *Only then can you exercise your authority as a believer.*

God's Word is the only power that will set a person free. God spoke His Word, and the earth and the heavens were created. God's Word spoken through your lips, in faith, has the same power and authority to set captives free.

Our Authority to Overcome and Rule

*Behold, I give you the authority to trample on ser-
pents and scorpions, and over all the power of the
enemy, and nothing shall by any means hurt you.*
—Luke 10:19

DURING THE LAST few years God has placed
urgency in our hearts to minister to people who
are living under all kinds of bondages. Satan has
a sinister plan already in action in these last days, and
many people, especially Christians, do not realize that
Satan is persecuting them. They presume that everything
that happens to them is meant to be, and they accept it
as part of their life. In many cases this includes persecution, oppression, sickness, and financial distress. Some
are under the false impression that Christians cannot be
oppressed by demons.

But, praise God, Jesus Christ paid a great price to
deliver us from the kingdom of darkness and translate

us into the kingdom of light! We now have authority to stand and resist the enemy and nothing shall harm us! Jesus defeated Satan on the cross of Calvary and transferred that authority to every believer (Luke 10:19).

These truths we share with you have changed the lives of many people, breaking severe bondages and releasing them to live in acceptance and love. When a broken person comes to an understanding of his or her identity in Christ, that person is set free from the hurts of the past. We believe these truths taken from the Word of God go beyond modern psychiatry, because not only do they localize the problem, but they also present a solution.

MAN IS A SPIRIT WITH A SOUL IN A BODY

Man is a spirit and has a soul and lives in a body. When we ignore this fact, we will find that man's approach to solving man's emotional problems is very inadequate or temporary.

Without any doubt we believe there are spiritual answers for the spiritual man. God's Spirit can reach down inside of man and bring forth a total unification where before there was separation caused by man.

Christ is our peace:

> For He Himself is our peace, who has made both one, and has broken down the middle wall of separation, having abolished in His flesh the enmity, that is, the law of commandments contained in ordinances, so as to create in Himself

one new man from the two, thus making peace,
and that He might reconcile them both to God
in one body through the cross, thereby putting
to death the enmity.

—EPHESIANS 2:14–16

Satan was defeated on the cross. He is a defeated foe
who has left his forces scattered in the land, and we, as
Christians, must take possession of our land back from
the control of Satan. To possess the land means to boldly
face the enemy and his works. There can be no compro-
mise in any area. The land of promise is the land of complete victory. This can be yours if you are willing to come
against all the works of the enemy.

WE CAN'T BLAME GOD OR THE DEVIL FOR ALL OUR SETBACKS

Now, we want to make one thing clear—we are not
demon hunters, and we certainly don't want anyone to
become one. Neither God nor Satan is responsible for all
the things that happen to man. We have a free will, and
many setbacks in our lives happen because we will for
them to happen. However, Satan does play a vital role
in every Christian's life, and the sooner you understand
this, the sooner you will have victory in your life. To
obtain this freedom, you must not only learn about the
authority you have over Satan, but you must also put it
into action constantly.

THE NAME OF JESUS CHRIST IS YOUR AUTHORITY

> Therefore God also has highly exalted Him and
> given Him the name which is above every name,
> that at the name of Jesus every knee should bow,
> of those in heaven, and of those on earth, and
> of those under the earth, and that every tongue
> should confess that Jesus Christ is Lord, to the
> glory of God the Father.
>
> —PHILIPPIANS 2:9–11

We must take Jesus's place and use Jesus's name just as
though Jesus Himself was present.

God has delegated this authority to us (Luke 9:1;
10:19). The authority of Christ as conqueror over all of
Satan's evil spirits is not a natural quality inherent in
every believer. Through the power of the Holy Spirit in
response to faith, the believer becomes empowered. The
degree of authority is determined by the degree of personal
victory the believer has in his own life.

> Then He called His twelve disciples together and
> gave them power and authority over all demons,
> and to cure diseases.
>
> —LUKE 9:1

Your degree of authority is determined by knowledge
and discernment and by what the Holy Spirit of God
reveals to you. You must have faith in the power of the
name of Jesus. Your faith is based on the knowledge you
attain of Christ and His works.

The blood of Jesus is your covering and your protection from Satan's attacks. His Spirit is your strength and power.

> But he who is joined to the Lord is one spirit with Him.
> —1 CORINTHIANS 6:17

> That He would grant you, according to the riches of His glory, to be strengthened with might through His Spirit in the inner man.
> —EPHESIANS 3:16

We have His ability and His power. How can we fail? These spiritual weapons must be released by faith through your mouth by prayer, confession, and your authority.

Whenever you feel burdened and attacked by circumstances, it could very possibly be an onslaught from the enemy. The devil's fierce attacks leave many believers feeling weak and unable to resist or to pray fearlessly. As you learn to put on the armor of God and understand that you are literally receiving and acknowledging that Jesus Christ lives in you and is your only God and Lord, you will begin to live and operate in victory, even in the midst of hellish attacks.

The authority of the believer is a privilege granted to us by God. Without authority a believer remains vulnerable to spiritual attacks from the kingdom of darkness. Many of God's people today need deliverance. We do not claim to be totally knowledgeable in every area of deliverance. But we feel an obligation to share with you some things we have learned that have helped scores of people in the past years through ministry. We offer these truths to you as a guide for healing and restoration of the body of Christ, believing that man can be a total man, free to relate to others and free to relate to his God.

RULE IN THE MIDST OF YOUR ENEMIES

God's Word to the church today is to "rule in the midst of your enemies" (Ps. 110:2, NIV). You must exercise the authority that Jesus purchased for you on the cross of Calvary when He defeated Satan and all his principalities. Assume your rightful position in the world as an overcomer doing the works of Jesus.

In general, many churches today have occupied a rather passive role in discipling believers in the area of their authority in Christ Jesus. God is saying to His church, "Rise up and rule in the midst of your enemies." The god of this world has established his strongholds and authorities in the land. *A defeated passive attitude will not conquer and possess.* Consequently the enemy remains in the land and God's people suffer. It is never God's will for His people to suffer from the oppression of the enemy.

God wants His people to be victorious—a strong army that can rule in the midst of circumstances rather than being ruled by circumstances. A people determined to do the will of God. A people who will seek the direction of the Holy Spirit rather than their own. Father God wants His children to magnify the name of the Lord—children who make the Lord their strong tower and their refuge.

> The challenge before the Christian today is to possess the land within—his soul.

He [God] has delivered us from the power of darkness and conveyed us into the kingdom of the Son of His love.

—COLOSSIANS 1:13

Satan's works must be met with a superior supernatural force—Christ Jesus in you.

To possess or dominate your soul, your mind, will, and emotions must be aligned with the Word of God. Your hope and expectation must be anchored in Christ. Only then can you exercise your dominion and authority in the name of Jesus. Salvation comes from God.

Truly my soul silently waits for God;
From Him comes my salvation.

—PSALM 62:1

Satan will always try to rob the provisions God gave to man. He will always challenge the believer.

DON'T ALLOW YOUR MIND TO BECOME PASSIVE

If you allow your mind to become passive and inactive, offering no resistance to the attacks of the enemy on your thought life, you will continue to dwell in darkness.

> Your thoughts will cause you to doubt or believe—to cringe back or move forward.

If a person will not use his intelligence, neither will God, but evil spirits will do so. Evil spirits require a blank mind and a passive will to bring people under all kinds of bondages. Passivity is overcome by activating the mind. Make a decision and confess, "I have the mind of Christ. I will not allow any outside force to employ or control my mind."

> For "who has known the mind of the LORD that he may instruct Him?" But we have the mind of Christ.
>
> —1 CORINTHIANS 2:16

Take the initiative in each action and word and do not depend on anyone else. Exercise your mind, and allow it to be guided by the Holy Spirit by thinking, reasoning, remembering, and understanding the sacrifice that Jesus made for you. Examine the source of your thoughts. Bring every thought captive to the obedience of Christ. Every believer is responsible to renew his own mind.

And do not be conformed to this world, but be transformed by the renewing of your mind, that you may prove what is that good and acceptable and perfect will of God.

—ROMANS 12:2

It is very important that you get your mind in tune with your spirit.

For to be carnally minded is death, but to be spiritually minded is life and peace. Because the carnal mind is enmity against God; for it is not subject to the law of God, nor indeed can be. So then, those who are in the flesh cannot please God. But you are not in the flesh but in the Spirit, if indeed the Spirit of God dwells in you. Now if anyone does not have the Spirit of Christ, he is not His.

—ROMANS 8:6–9

To be transformed by the renewing of your mind means to arrive at the highest possibility that God has ordained for man's mind. Satan will make it seem like a huge task, and for some, it may seem like an impossible commitment, but God has delivered us from the power of darkness. He has enabled and wired us in such a unique way that we can be transformed by willfully allowing our minds to be renewed by the Word of God.

It may sound like an uphill struggle, but believe us, one step at a time, one Bible verse at a time, one prayer at a time, one no at a time, and you will start noticing a transformation take place. God has conveyed us into His kingdom. A change of ownership has taken place. We can do this! We have authority!

The Definition of Authority

Authority is power that is exercised by rulers or others in high positions by virtue of their office. (See Ephesians 1:20–23; 3:10; 6:12.) Authority can also be defined as, "the right to command, power given over somebody, justification, permission, legitimate power, a quality that is respected."

Satan has an influence over man's will, causing him to do things displeasing to God. Man's will is his organ for decision making. According to Ephesians 1:17–23 and Colossians 2:15, the church today has a mandate to rule with Christ in the midst of His enemies.

Why do you think God made His power available to believers? Just so we could wear the label of "powerful Spirit-filled Christians"? No! No! God gave us authority so that we can remain free and set other people free from the strongholds of the enemy.

Satan's strategy is to deceive us into believing that we are not qualified to bring down his strongholds. He also deceives many people by causing them to believe that they have to spend years in Bible schools and seminaries before they can even lay hands on the sick and ask God to heal them.

Every minister of God needs training and knowledge

about what the Bible says about spiritual warfare and our authority in the name of Jesus. We must believe that God's power to defeat evil spirits is also active and operating in a believer's life.

> And when He had called His twelve disciples to Him, He gave them power over unclean spirits, to cast them out, and to heal all kinds of sickness and all kinds of disease.
>
> —MATTHEW 10:1

4

THE POWER OF SPIRITUAL ARMOR AND THE WORD OF GOD

*Finally, my brethren, be strong in the Lord
and in the power of His might. Put on the
whole armor of God, that you may be able
to stand against the wiles of the devil.*

—Ephesians 6:10–11

THE WORD CLEARLY states that we are not to be ignorant of Satan's devices—yet many remain ignorant, allowing Satan to continually destroy their homes, steal their possessions, and ruin their health while they helplessly wonder what they did wrong. The reason for this is that many Christians do not know that they have been given authority over all the power of the enemy to prevent his attacks. And for some, when they become aware of their authority, they fail to exercise it.

We must face the fact that we need to prepare ourselves

and be ready to confront the many demonic challenges constantly confronting us.

THE ABSOLUTE IMPORTANCE OF PUTTING ON THE ARMOR OF GOD

Before we go into the area of spiritual warfare, deliverance, and our authority to resist Satan, we must remember one thing—Satan has had more than six thousand years of experience in persecuting and tormenting Christians. *If you go into battle to resist Satan without the full armor of God, you are defeated before you start.* This is what is happening to so many Christians today—they try to do warfare with the forces of darkness without the protection of their spiritual armor. The armor is not very comfortable to put on, but it is very necessary if you want to be effective. It's not a call to war but a declaration to live in victory. Paul's instructions to the Ephesians—and us—about the armor are very specific and powerful:

> Therefore, put on every piece of God's armor so you will be able to resist the enemy in the time of evil. Then after the battle you will still be standing firm. Stand your ground, putting on the belt of truth and the body armor of God's righteousness. For shoes, put on the peace that comes from the Good News so that you will be fully prepared. In addition to all of these, hold up the shield of faith to stop the fiery arrows of the devil. Put on salvation as your helmet, and take the sword of the Spirit, which is the word of

God. Pray in the Spirit at all times and on every occasion. Stay alert and be persistent in your prayers for all believers everywhere.

—Ephesians 6:13–18, nlt

The belt of truth

"Stand your ground, putting on the belt of truth" (v. 14, nlt). A Roman soldier in Paul's day wore a leather girdle around his waist to protect his loins and to carry weapons, such as a sword. A policeman today also has weapons attached to his belt, such as a gun and handcuffs. The belt holds the weapons in place close to the body. The belt can be likened to your integrity, honesty, and truth. Speaking truth is speaking God's Word. When you declare and confess the Word, you are putting on the belt of truth.

The breastplate of righteousness

Putting on the breastplate of righteousness is important because Satan always goes after a man's heart and his conscience. Your righteousness in Christ will defeat Satan every time. It is one of God's attributes imputed to you upon salvation. Your filthiness is exchanged for His righteousness. The breastplate gives you confidence and assurance in the process of sanctification.

Shoes of peace

"For shoes, put on the peace that comes from the Good News so that you will be fully prepared" (v. 15, nlt). The peace of God gives you a firm footing. Many believers walk around without peace, miserably believing that's part of their cross to bear in life. None of us are immune to trials and tribulations. Darkness and fear attack all of us. But we must be careful not to confess or express all our fears. The enemy looks for your confession so that he can have a right to attack you. You must instead confess God's Word and stand firm in your peace. It is a necessary part of the armor. Peace of mind in the midst of trouble is warfare at its best. It is a position you must take. God has promised to never forsake us. Christ gave us His peace.

The shield of faith

"Hold up the shield of faith to stop the fiery arrows of the devil" (v. 14, NLT). Your faith is a shield from all of the enemy's fiery darts and assaults. The shield of faith is God's sovereign omnipresence in your life. God is "your shield, your exceedingly great reward" (Gen. 15:1). God requires your daily dependence and communion with Him and His Spirit. Just like food, it becomes your daily sustenance and your very life. You must hold up your shield of faith every day and confess and declare your union with Christ. He is your covering.

The helmet of salvation

"Put on salvation as your helmet" (Eph. 6:17, NLT). The purpose of a helmet is to protect the head. In this scripture the purpose of your helmet as part of the armor is to protect your mind from the lies of the enemy. We are in a spiritual war. Father God knows that without your constant surveillance of your thoughts, you can become double-minded, and you know how much God hates double mindedness. A mind controlled by the Spirit of God produces life and peace (Rom. 8:6–7). Keep the devil's thoughts out of your mind by putting on the mind of Christ. You do this by studying and meditating on the Word. Christ Jesus is your salvation. This piece of the armor, the helmet of salvation, is also Christ in you!

The sword of the Spirit

"Take the sword of the Spirit, which is the word of God" (Eph. 6:17, NLT). Taking in the Word is taking in spiritual food. Without it you will remain anemic, debilitated, and unable to lift up the sword of the Spirit to confront an intruding enemy. No Word; no power. More Word, more confidence and fire in your bones. The living Word is an offensive weapon. The moment you lift up the sword of the Spirit and speak a scripture into an adverse situation, the enemy has to take his hands off. This kind of belief takes fearlessness and practice.

Speak to your mountains. Speak the Word to your sickness. Use your sword every day. Make sure all the other parts of your armor are in place. Your spiritual man must be in order and ready for the battle. It's easier than you may think. It takes a willingness to surrender all to the Master. Living by faith and believing God must become a lifestyle. Only then will you enjoy peace and victory in this life. The applied Word of God heals and restores as it penetrates deeply, removing all the garbage inflicted by past experiences and false teachings.

The person of the Holy Spirit is the one wielding your sword of the Spirit. Without the Holy Spirit you have no effective sword. You must be controlled by the Spirit to be effective in warfare. Satan has to retreat when you appropriately use the sword of the Spirit, the Word of God.

Pray in the Spirit

"Pray in the Spirit at all times and on every occasion. Stay alert and be persistent in your prayers for all believers everywhere" (v. 18, NLT). Prayer is what keeps this entire armor in place. Without prayer and communication with God we become loners, separated from God and His love. As we remain in relationship with Christ, connected with the Holy Spirit, clothed in God's armor, and committed to a prayer lifestyle, we become invincible in the face of the enemy. No evil force can remain in our atmosphere. Perseverance in prayer will help you conquer the lustful desires of your flesh. Without consistent fervent prayers you will not be able to win your battles. The prayers of a righteous man or woman are powerful and effective (James 5:16). Your powerful prayers will cause God to perform His Word in your life.

PRAYER TO PUT ON THE ARMOR OF GOD

Father God, I thank You for the protection You have provided for me through my right standing with Christ.

I put on the belt of truth for protection over my personal life and my loved ones. Place a hunger in me for the truth in the Word of God. Help me to never be deceived by the lies of the enemy. Help me to always walk in integrity.

I put on the breastplate of righteousness. Thank You, Holy Spirit, for Your indwelling power that helps me to remain steadfast in my words, thoughts, and actions. I realize that my success depends on my remaining steadfast in my calling as a child of God. I refuse to remain passive, knowing that my victory rests in Christ Jesus taking first place in my life.

I put on the shoes of peace. Thank You, Lord, for Your promise in John 14:27, "Peace I leave with you, My peace I give to you." I will not be afraid, knowing that Your peace is always with me.

Father, You surround the righteous with Your shield of favor (Ps. 5:12). Your protection gives me confidence that no matter what the battle brings, You will uphold me with Your righteous right hand.

I hold up the shield of faith, believing that Your divine intervention is always near me. It is You, Jehovah, who lovingly interferes with all of Satan's sinister strategies against me. I stand confident that Your power is greater than the power of the enemy. I exercise my faith and resist the devil with confidence that he must flee.

I now put on my helmet of salvation to withstand all the flaming attacks and lies of the enemy against my mind and my thoughts. Thank You, Lord Jesus, because You willingly became our salvation, and I can boldly declare that I have the mind of Christ (1 Cor. 2:16).

I take hold of the sword of the Spirit, which is the Word of God. Thank You, Holy Spirit, for teaching me how to study and meditate on the Word of God. Thank You for revealing wisdom and understanding. Help me to remain disciplined and committed to the study of Your Word. The Word of God is alive and powerful and sharper than a two-edged sword, setting me free from the strongholds of the enemy (Heb. 4:12).

I will pray in the Spirit at all times. Holy Spirit, I desire to pray in the Spirit and be able to do it at all times. Thank You for teaching me how to stay focused and know when the enemy seeks to interfere in my life. You have promised never to leave us or forsake us. I choose to obey Your Word and to be led by Your Spirit. I take back all ground I conceded to the enemy by my sins and transgressions and through ignorance. I draw near to You, Holy Spirit, and I thank You for teaching me how to pray in the Spirit. In Jesus's wonderful name, amen.

> In simple words, the armor described in Ephesians 6 is Jesus Christ in us.

TRANSFORMED BY THE WORD OF GOD

The Word of God is so powerful that it can transform a degenerated man into a new man. This would be impossible through human influence or power. Peter confirmed this when he wrote, "Having been born again, not of corruptible seed but incorruptible, through the word of God which lives and abides forever" (1 Pet. 1:23).

The following scriptures affirm the importance of being transformed by God's Word. Consider the degree to which you are applying each of these spiritual principles to your own spiritual transformation.

1. The Word purifies my heart and my soul.

Sanctify them by Your truth. Your Word is truth.
—JOHN 17:17

Husbands, love your wives, just as Christ also loved the church and gave Himself for her, that He might sanctify and cleanse her with the washing of water by the word, that He might present her to Himself a glorious church, not having spot or wrinkle or any such thing.

—EPHESIANS 5:25–27

2. The Word is powerful and able to heal me.

He sent His word and healed them,
And delivered them from their destructions.

—PSALM 107:20

For they are life to those who find them,
And health to all their flesh.

—PROVERBS 4:22

3. The Word gives me life.

Most assuredly, I say to you, he who hears My word and believes in Him who sent Me has everlasting life, and shall not come into judgment, but has passed from death into life.

—JOHN 5:24

4. The Word I believe is able to revive me.

Though I walk in the midst of trouble, You will
    revive me;
You will stretch out Your hand

Against the wrath of my enemies,
And Your right hand will save me.

—PSALM 138:7

5. The Word comforts and gives me unwavering hope.

For whatever things were written before were written for our learning, that we through the patience and comfort of the Scriptures might have hope.

—ROMANS 15:4

In the beginning God spoke and created the heavens and the earth. God has given us dominion and authority to speak His Word and see results. By faith we can command evil spirits, sickness, disease, and all demonic interruptions to depart from us and our substance, and they must obey. The same words spoken by our lips in faith have the same power and potential as Jesus's words had.

THE CHRISTIAN VS. EVIL SPIRITS

Deliverance from evil spirits is one of the most controversial subjects among Christians. The question in people's minds is, "Can a Christian be possessed by demons?"

This question arose years ago when some denominational churches began to teach that born-again believers could not be possessed with demons. This was true to a point. But the problem was that they ended their teaching there and left out the most important aspect of the subject, which is: *Christians can be oppressed, burdened, and afflicted by demons.*

The enemy would like nothing better than for us to believe that demons cannot influence the life of a born-again believer. This is one of Satan's subtle ways of deceiving people's lives. He causes Christians to believe they are immune to demonic attacks. Satan uses his demons to wreck their lives in the process.

Many Christians live under different stages of fear, oppression, bondage, sickness, poverty, or total defeat. God ordained for believers to live under the faith covenant and to enjoy peace, love, joy, divine health, abundance, and victory.

Nothing can be found in the Word to confirm that all evil spirits are expelled automatically when a person receives salvation. The demons in a person's body at the time of salvation just become dormant for a period of time. If the person does not grow spiritually, they will remain inactive.

When the believer strives for a deeper walk with God, these demons will become active according to the person's degree of commitment and will cause problems until they are finally driven out. Demons do not want a person to become a Christian in the first place, much less see them commit to the Lord all the way. Demons do not want believers to become *overcomers* who will resist them, but they don't seem to mind a carnal Christian.

Can Demons Possess the Spirit of a Born-Again Believer?

When you have had a true born-again experience of salvation with Jesus, demons cannot penetrate your spirit, because God dwells there. They cannot keep you from entering heaven.

But though demons can and do cause believers to become defeated by attacking their soul, mind, and body, God has provided weapons of spiritual warfare to counteract every attack of the enemy.

Many in the body of Christ have a defeated attitude in the face of the enemy who rules this world. As we stated earlier, we believe it is time to listen to what God is saying to His church: "Rule in the midst of Your enemies!" (Ps. 110:2). If you continue displaying a defeated attitude, you will not be able to conquer the enemy. He will remain in your territory, and you will continue to suffer in a great way. But as you exercise your authority, you become an overcomer—a strong and valiant soldier in God's army.

God has given you the power and the choice to walk in freedom so that you can claim all of your possessions out of the control of Satan. In order to remain free, you must abide by God's Word and believe what it says—that you "are more than conquerors" (Rom. 8:37).

Jesus Died to Defeat Satan

When Jesus died on the cross, He not only shed His blood for our sins and suffered His stripes for our healing, but He also totally defeated Satan. At this time Jesus transferred His authority over Satan to every believer on this earth. We must use this delegated power to keep Satan and his demons out of our lives so that we can readily adhere to God's directions through the Holy Spirit. God is the eternal power over the enemy, and He made this power available to us through Jesus. But if we do not use this power, we cannot expect to receive many blessings.

Jesus defeated Satan and his demons on the cross, but their full sentence has not been carried out yet. God gave us, as believers, the privilege and the responsibility of announcing to Satan and his demons their defeat in our lives and the lives of others.

PRAYER TO RECEIVE FREEDOM FROM THE POWER OF THE ENEMY

Father God, I rejoice knowing the truth that Satan is a defeated foe and that Christ Jesus has given me authority over all the power of the enemy as I stand committed and obedient to Your Word.

I refuse to walk in fear and remain a victim of circumstances. I declare that I belong to the kingdom of God, and I am a partaker of all of Your blessings. I take by force what belongs to me and aggressively loose myself from all inherited strongholds, sickness, disease, and addictions. I loose the peace and healing power of God to invade my life and heal my mind and body, in the name of Jesus. Amen.

Recognizing the Enemy's Strategy

5

The Flesh and Evil Spirits

*Therefore if the Son makes you
free, you shall be free indeed.*

—John 8:36

A YOUNG EVANGELIST CAME to visit our home a
few years ago. He needed counsel. His ministry
was thriving and many people were receiving
Christ. He devoted many hours each day to studying the
Word and preparing himself for ministry. Large crowds
attended his meetings, intrigued by his fearlessness of
evil spirits and the ministry of deliverance. His deep
concern was that he had an unbridled temper, let loose
when his wife or children would disagree with him. In
his teenage years he had become a gang member whose
main identifying purpose was to gouge out an eye of
other rival gang members who did them harm. For that
purpose the gang member would grow a long and sharp
fingernail.

As we carefully listened and observed this young and well-presented evangelist in his midthirties, we noticed his pinky finger was long and sharply pointed. Curiosity got the best of my wife, Iris, and she asked him why he still had a long sharp nail. His answer was that it had become a habit, and even though he had cut it off several times, he found himself growing it again. *Therein was the secret to his unbridled anger.* He confessed that when he got angry at his wife, a desire would well up in his heart to gouge out one of her eyes.

God gave us a specific word for this man. I (John) was led by the Spirit of the Lord to tell him that this was his last opportunity to surrender completely to God, receive deliverance, cut off his nail, and begin blessing his family, or the hand of the Lord would allow him to end up in a wheelchair. Now that's a tough and direct word. He agreed to come back another day soon to go through the process of deliverance. He never did. A year later we met him while he was recovering in a wheelchair, the result of lashing out with angry words at four guys who beat him almost to death. His wife had left him, and his son had turned to the homosexual lifestyle.

There was so much blessing waiting for this young minister, and so much authority from God to defeat satanic oppression. Yet there was also opposition and a war in his spirit to surrender all to God for the freedom to be found only in Christ Jesus. He ended up in a spiritual wheelchair as well as a physical one. Even though he can rise up and start fresh, the consequences are real. Studying God's Word is not enough. Praying is not enough. Our obedience and surrender are better than all the sacrifices we can ever make (1 Sam. 15:22).

It is God's desire that we live free from mental torment, fear, jealousy, hatred, lust, pride, self-pity, addictions, gluttony, and all other forms of bondage, oppression, and defilement.

The truth is that there is a battle raging every day in the spiritual realm. The battle is for your faith and your heart. Most Christians are aware of this intense warfare, but honestly, they don't realize they must take some steps of action and vigilance to aggressively resist demonic interference. The first step is to realize that to live free we must engage and participate in guarding the gates of our heart and our senses.

Every choice you make, every action you take, every thought you process, and every word you say will determine whether God or Satan will have dominion in your life. Satan cannot affect your life without your consent. God cannot bless you without your allegiance to Him. The key to remain in freedom is to recognize that you are in a constant battle for your soul, and you must remain steadfast and submitted to your Lord and Savior, Jesus Christ.

> Therefore submit to God. Resist the devil and he will flee from you.
>
> —James 4:7

THE FLESH AND EVIL SPIRITS

There are two main causes for man's inner problems: The first is the *flesh* or the *old man*. This is man's carnal unregenerate, rebellious nature, which is influenced and buffeted by Satan. The second cause of the inner problems is *evil spirits*—Satan's angels, which he uses to bind some aspect of the *flesh* and which WILL NOT relinquish their hold unless compelled to do so.

Every Christian who is almost totally ignorant of the nature of evil spirits will become fearful of things beyond his understanding and choose to ignore this portion of God's ministry. Too many believers have not been taught the importance of their authority over Satan, and as a result, multitudes of precious Christians are living in needless torment today. Much of the ministry of Christ was devoted to casting devils out of tormented people. This should also be a vital part of our ministry today.

> And these signs will follow those who believe: In My name they will cast out demons.
> —MARK 16:17

> And the multitudes with one accord heeded the things spoken by Philip, hearing and seeing the miracles which he did. For unclean spirits, crying with a loud voice, came out of many who were possessed; and many who were paralyzed and lame were healed.
> —ACTS 8:6–7

It's a pity that so many people attribute all personal problems to the activity of evil spirits. This is untrue because we have been created with a free will. When we willfully do things that are displeasing to God and that harm the temple of God, then we have to suffer the consequences. We cannot blame it on God or Satan.

It is important that every sincere believer totally renounces all evil in his life, makes a personal commitment to God, and be directed by the Holy Spirit. When you are not willing to meet this requirement, there can be no permanent solution to your problem.

HABITS AND PRACTICES THAT ATTRACT EVIL SPIRITS

The following list reveals some of the areas that attract evil spirits to take residency in your life. To live free, you must confess and renounce all sinful habits that invite and give entry to evil spirits.

Attitude problems

One main area of conflict in a person's life is attitude. A bad attitude may lead to all types of mental disturbances. The word *attitude* in this context means: "boldness, brashness, arrogance, insolence, defiance, and assertiveness." A bad attitude may lead to rebellion. Evil spirits thrive in an atmosphere of rebellion. Attitude problems usually begin in infancy. When a child is allowed to display rebellion of any kind, it eventually spreads to every area of their interpersonal relationships.

Insatiable desires

This area of uncontrolled appetites and insatiable desires affects people from all walks of life and has become an epidemic all around the world. When unrestrained desires are allowed to continue without self-control, the door is opened for the influence of evil spirits, which may develop into addictions to food, alcohol, tobacco, medications, drugs, romance books and novels, shopping, cruelty, hatred, rebellion, and other things.

Religious beliefs

Religious practices, obsessions, and experiences that involve contact with the spirit world, channeling, worship of idols, occult practices, and other forms of worship that deny the death and resurrection of Jesus Christ as Lord and Savior can drive a person to commit sinful acts that become curses, affecting not only a family but also generations to come.

Sexual obsessions

Sexual immorality can lead a person to obsessive sexual urges, perversion, abuse, and the like. It is no secret that all over the world sexual abuse has become so prevalent and of such widespread proportions that most people who watch the news or hear someone talk about it seem to dismiss it with an "Oh well, what else is new?" Sadly, the victim remains wounded forever, unless he or she receives help and mercy. Millions of sexually abused people experience some kind of obsessive habit. Some of the most obvious obsessions today are Internet pornography, sexting, masturbation, fornication, adultery, child porn, and many other forms of sexual obsession.

To receive freedom, the individual must confess, renounce, repent, and forgive—and then follow up with a renewing of the mind and Bible-based discipleship.

HOMOSEXUALITY AND SEXUAL ADDICTIONS

God did not create homosexuals or sex addicts.

> So God created man in His own image; in the image of God He created him; male and female He created them.
>
> —GENESIS 1:27

Homosexuality is a result of rebellion against God.

> Therefore God also gave them up to uncleanness, in the lusts of their hearts, to dishonor their bodies among themselves, who exchanged the truth of God for the lie, and worshiped and served the creature rather than the Creator, who is blessed forever. Amen. For this reason God gave them up to vile passions. For even their women exchanged the natural use for what is against nature. Likewise also the men, leaving the natural use of the woman, burned in their lust for one another, men with men committing what is shameful, and receiving in themselves the penalty of their error which was due.
>
> —ROMANS 1:24–27

It is important to know what the Bible says about homosexuality:

> You shall not lie with a male as with a woman. It is an abomination.
>
> —LEVITICUS 18:22

> If a man lies with a male as he lies with a woman, both of them have committed an abomination. They shall surely be put to death. Their blood shall be upon them.
>
> —LEVITICUS 20:13

> Do you not know that the unrighteous will not inherit the kingdom of God? Do not be deceived. Neither fornicators, nor idolaters, nor adulterers, nor homosexuals, nor sodomites, nor thieves, nor covetous, nor drunkards, nor revilers, nor extortioners will inherit the kingdom of God.
>
> —1 CORINTHIANS 6:9–10

Homosexuality may be caused by many reasons.

Parents can inadvertently influence a child to develop abnormal behavior. It may be the influence of a mother who desired to have a girl but instead had a boy. In her passion and ignorance she dresses the boy as a girl. The child grows up with a confused identity and continues liking to dress as a girl. Or perhaps a mother constantly treats a son as a *mama's boy*, protecting him from everything and not allowing him to develop normally. A father who never gives attention, love, or blessings to his children can create rejection toward the opposite sex, unless there is an attentive mother aware of the child's needs. Sexual abuse is one of the most prevalent causes. Various circumstances in life may cause spirits of trauma and confusion to influence a young mind, such as:

- Visual and provocative sexual images

- Abnormal relationships

- Sexual abuse and molestation

- Rejection and self-rejection

- Resentment, hateful words

- Hatred, fears

There will always be the issue of rebellion when a young person goes against his or her good upbringing and even the prayers of parents and decides to mess with sin and forsake instruction and everything that represents right and wrong.

What does a parent do then? Stand firm and unwavering upon God's Word, resist the enemy in prayer, and love your son or daughter with every fiber in your being. Understand that your child's salvation is the most important issue in his or her life. Don't be moved by what you see, hear, and know. Use your authority in the name of Jesus against all the wiles of the enemy to disarm spiritual blindness, and continue trusting God. Your faith and your love will keep a hook of salvation attached to your loved one.

THE INFLUENCE OF DECEIVING SPIRITS

During this writing, one of my (Iris) intercessors and dear friends shared her testimony of divine intervention. She's a single mom with an adult son who shares her home. For several months she noticed a shifting in her son's routine and a disinterest in church attendance. He became distant and distraught. One day she received an e-mail from a friend whose son is friends with her son. There was an attachment in the e-mail of a message my intercessor's son shared with his friend. That message was her son's intent to commit suicide. Reading it shook up my friend, and she immediately confronted her son, asking him why he had those feelings. He had no specific explanation and was unable to open up to his mom.

Instead of agonizing and becoming fearful, she did what every child of God should do in a similar situation with a loved one. *She surrendered at her altar,* beseeching God on behalf of her son. Something was wrong. Some demonic entity had penetrated her son's mind, and she wasn't about to let it steal what belonged to her. Warfare praying took over. The weapons of binding and loosing were initiated. A battle for the life of her son ensued, and angels were placed on assignment. My friend knew that her prayers were powerful to the pulling down of strongholds and every evil spirit instigating and deceiving her son.

That same day, after hours of warring in the Spirit, the answer came. She moved quickly, followed the leading of the Holy Spirit, and entered her son's room. She didn't hear the audible voice of the Spirit, but she knew in her spirit what she needed to do. She opened the closet door, stooped down, and took out a small suitcase. She cautiously opened it and felt around in its contents. Her hand suddenly grasped something that felt like a book. She pulled it out, opened it, and immediately knew she was holding a Wicca bible. This is it, she thought—this is the stronghold!

When her son came home, she confronted him with the bible. He explained that the mother of one of his friends had given it to him. Upon further inquiry my friend found out that the woman was a witch. Now, the reason I'm sharing this testimony is because it paints a picture of what could happen when a person dabbles and gets involved with anything that belongs to the kingdom of darkness. It's no game. It's very real. Satan's kingdom is very well organized. It is a hierarchy with many levels of organization and leadership.

This mom proceeded to destroy the Wicca bible, cancel the demonic assignment of death by suicide against her son, and deliver him from a premature death.

The kingdom of God is at hand. Every believer has authority over every demonic stronghold. But just as a car without gasoline is going nowhere, so it is with a believer who has authority to resist the enemy and also intercede for God's deliverance, but instead becomes fearful and anxious. He will never see or experience the victories and freedom available to him. Today my friend has much to thank God for. Her son's blinders have come off his eyes and the veil has been removed from his heart.

The Bible reveals that *deceiving spirits* may seduce a child of God away from the protection of the blood of Jesus, entice him to miss God's will for his life, and lead him to death and self-destruction. When Satan and his demonic spirits manage to control some area of a believer's life, he may become confused and defeated and must seek help.

> Now the Spirit expressly says that in latter times some will depart from the faith, giving heed to deceiving spirits and doctrines of demons.
> —1 TIMOTHY 4:1

THE IMPORTANCE OF CONFESSION AND FORGIVENESS

Humility, honesty, and a willingness to confess all known sin and to turn from all sin and contact with evil spirits are absolutely necessary to obtain complete freedom.

Forgiveness of all people involved and complete surrender to the Lordship of Jesus Christ in every area of your life is very crucial. You must be willing to completely surrender to God to remain free.

Your body becomes the temple of God when Christ Jesus becomes your Lord and Savior. When your sign displays *VACANCY*, demons are free to enter because Christ is no longer present. When you are born again, your sign on the temple says *NO VACANCY*, and they cannot enter unless you allow them to do so.

AN ACTIVE WILL

An active will is necessary to maintain deliverance in every area of life. When your will is in control of your spirit, mind, and body, you are guaranteed freedom. There is no substitute for repentance. There is no substitute for self-discipline.

- We must be fearless aggressors against the enemy.

- The enemy only respects someone who is more powerful than he.

- Spiritual force must be used against spiritual force.

As we approach the end of this age, Jesus said that men's hearts would fail them for fear of things that are coming on this earth. Therefore we need to use all the power and authority we have received from Christ so that we can walk and live in peace and liberty here on earth.

To be a disciple of Christ, you must be separated from the world. You must live your Christianity and not just talk about it. We are chosen people of God. He has given us specific authority and privileges to live in the kingdom of heaven right here on earth.

To demonstrate your love toward God, you must put your faith into action and live victoriously. You need to be careful not to jeopardize your inheritance by joining the multitudes of mouth-professing Christians who live under condemnation instead of faith in God Almighty. Your will must always remain actively involved by obeying God's precepts and commandments.

For a deeper understanding of how to receive freedom and healing from abusive or traumatic experiences, sickness, or a poor understanding about salvation, we highly recommend Iris Delgado's book *Satan, You Can't Have My Miracle*, published by Charisma House.

6

THE BATTLE FOR YOUR MIND

*But I see another law in my members, warring
against the law of my mind, and bringing me into captivity to the law of sin which is in my members.*

—Romans 7:23

THIS CHAPTER WILL introduce you to many of the
principles you must understand about your mind
and Satan's desire to hinder you from avoiding his
insidious progressive takeover of it. Each principle will
provide you with a scriptural support.

Many of these principles may be concepts or issues
that are affecting your own life. Determine to do a
deeper study of these principles so that you may achieve
victory over Satan's strategies and walk in freedom from
his demonic control.

Anything the mind sets itself on and accepts is what man will desire and seek after.

> Do you not know that to whom you present yourselves slaves to obey, you are that one's slaves whom you obey, whether of sin leading to death, or of obedience leading to righteousness?
> —Romans 6:16

A disturbed mind is harmful to the spiritual life.

> And even as they did not like to retain God in their knowledge, God gave them over to a debased mind, to do those things which are not fitting.
> —Romans 1:28

Your mind should not to be ruled by your feelings.

> A fool vents all his feelings,
> But a wise man holds them back.
> —Proverbs 29:11

Your head needs to be kept in a humble state.

> Be of the same mind toward one another. Do not set your mind on high things, but associate with the humble. Do not be wise in your own opinion.
> —Romans 12:16

The Word of God must be implanted into your mind.

> Therefore lay aside all filthiness and overflow of wickedness, and receive with meekness the implanted word, which is able to save your souls.
>
> —JAMES 1:21

Your mind must not operate independently of the Spirit's rule.

> For those who live according to the flesh set their minds on the things of the flesh, but those who live according to the Spirit, the things of the Spirit.
>
> —ROMANS 8:5

You are commanded to love God with all of your mind.

> "And you shall love the LORD your God with all your heart, with all your soul, with all your mind, and with all your strength." This is the first commandment.
>
> —MARK 12:30

We were created to be perfectly joined together in the same mind and in the same judgment.

> …that you be perfectly joined together in the same mind and in the same judgment.
>
> —1 CORINTHIANS 1:10

You were created with the mind of Christ.

> For "who has known the mind of the Lord that he may instruct Him?" But we have the mind of Christ.
>
> —1 Corinthians 2:16

The carnal mind is enmity against God and doesn't desire the things of the Spirit of God.

> Because the carnal mind is enmity against God; for it is not subject to the law of God, nor indeed can be.
>
> —Romans 8:7

God created our mind with the capacity to understand the spiritual principles of the kingdom of God. The Word says, "Be renewed in the spirit of your mind" (Eph. 4:23). This is a command. I believe it is the most important requirement that you must obey in order to exercise your authority over Satan and live in freedom.

God's truth defeats the lies of the enemy against the character of God and the devil's deception about who you are in Christ and your commitment to serve Him. (See John 8:44.) God's truth also enables you to enter into battle. To "gird up your loins" means to buckle your belt for action (1 Pet. 1:13). Be prepared for attack. (See also Exodus 12:11; Luke 12:35.)

The mind is the battleground of our thoughts. The mind governed by the flesh produces spiritual death. The mind governed by the Spirit of God produces life and peace.

> The mind of sinful man is death, but the mind controlled by the Spirit is life and peace.
>
> —ROMANS 8:6, NIV

The unrenewed mind remains and dwells in darkness.

> Whose minds the god of this age has blinded, who do not believe, lest the light of the gospel of the glory of Christ, who is the image of God, should shine on them.
>
> —2 CORINTHIANS 4:4

> …having their understanding darkened, being alienated from the life of God, because of the ignorance that is in them, because of the hardening of their heart…
>
> —EPHESIANS 4:18

FINDING FREEDOM FOR YOUR MIND

Your memory must be set free and cleansed from things of the past. Bondage in the mind from occult practices and false cults must be broken and forsaken. Every unclean thought has to be taken captive to the obedience of Christ.

The mind is a great battlefield; until every thought is

brought into captivity to the obedience of Christ, there can be no peace (2 Cor. 10:5).

A passive mind permits your reasoning powers to stay in a fixed position. If you do not use your intelligence, neither will God, but the evil spirits will because they require a blank brain and a passive will.

Love the Lord your God...with all your mind.
—MARK 12:30

7

THE PRINCIPLES OF SATAN'S OPPRESSION

*Because of the multitude of oppres-
sions the people cry out; they cry for help
because of the violence of the mighty.*

—Job 35:9, AMP

THE WORD OF God clearly identifies who our enemy is, how he came to be, and how he operates to attack and oppress mankind. The best way for the Christian to prepare for spiritual warfare against Satan and his forces—and to be victorious—is to thoroughly understand the principles of Satan's oppression and the weapons of warfare available to all believers. You must *know the enemy*—understanding how he works—if you want to live a victorious life. Ignorance will keep a child of God living a defeated life.

The next two chapters are filled with comprehensive information that will help you know your enemy. We recommend that you use this study and continue your analysis on this subject to sharpen your spiritual warfare tools. Remember that we are in this world, but we are not of this world. When we see things happening that are wrong and evil, remember it's not happening in the kingdom of God we live in. The worldly kingdom is limited, but we live in a kingdom that is unlimited. Keep things separated and in perspective. We are citizens of the kingdom of God. I will seek first the kingdom of God and His righteousness, and I believe that everything I need will be added unto me. (See Matthew 6:33.)

SATAN'S ORIGIN, FALL, AND FINAL DESTINY

The son of the morning is cast out.

> How you are fallen from heaven,
> O Lucifer, son of the morning!
> How you are cut down to the ground,
> You who weakened the nations!
> —ISAIAH 14:12

The anointed cherub of protection is cast out.

> You were the seal of perfection,
> Full of wisdom and perfect in beauty.
> You were in Eden, the garden of God;
> Every precious stone was your covering:
> The sardius, topaz, and diamond,
> Beryl, onyx, and jasper,
> Sapphire, turquoise, and emerald with gold.

The workmanship of your timbrels and pipes
Was prepared for you on the day you were created.

You were the anointed cherub who covers;
I established you;
You were on the holy mountain of God;
You walked back and forth in the midst of fiery
    stones.
You were perfect in your ways from the day you
    were created,
Till iniquity was found in you.

By the abundance of your trading
You became filled with violence within,
And you sinned;
Therefore I cast you as a profane thing
Out of the mountain of God;
And I destroyed you, O covering cherub,
From the midst of the fiery stones.

Your heart was lifted up because of your beauty;
You corrupted your wisdom for the sake of your
    splendor;
I cast you to the ground,
I laid you before kings,
That they might gaze at you.

You defiled your sanctuaries
By the multitude of your iniquities,
By the iniquity of your trading;
Therefore I brought fire from your midst;
It devoured you,

And I turned you to ashes upon the earth
In the sight of all who saw you.
All who knew you among the peoples are
    astonished at you;
You have become a horror,
And shall be no more forever.

—EZEKIEL 28:12–19

Satan falls from heaven as lightning.

And He said to them, "I saw Satan fall like
lightning from heaven. Behold, I give you the
authority to trample on serpents and scorpions,
and over all the power of the enemy, and nothing
shall by any means hurt you."

—LUKE 10:18–19

**The devil was destroyed by the death and resurrection
of Christ.**

Inasmuch then as the children have partaken of
flesh and blood, He Himself likewise shared in
the same, that through death He might destroy
him who had the power of death, that is, the
devil, and release those who through fear of
death were all their lifetime subject to bondage.

—HEBREWS 2:14–15

…having wiped out the handwriting of requirements that was against us, which was contrary to us. And He has taken it out of the way,
having nailed it to the cross. Having disarmed

principalities and powers, He made a public spectacle of them, triumphing over them in it.

—Colossians 2:14–15

Jesus Christ destroys the works of the devil.

He who sins is of the devil, for the devil has sinned from the beginning. For this purpose the Son of God was manifested, that He might destroy the works of the devil.

—1 John 3:8

The dragon, the serpent, and all the demons are cast out.

So the great dragon was cast out, that serpent of old, called the Devil and Satan, who deceives the whole world; he was cast to the earth, and his angels were cast out with him. Then I heard a loud voice saying in heaven, "Now salvation, and strength, and the kingdom of our God, and the power of His Christ have come, for the accuser of our brethren, who accused them before our God day and night, has been cast down. And they overcame him by the blood of the Lamb and by the word of their testimony, and they did not love their lives to the death."

—Revelation 12:9–11

The devil will be bound and thrown into the bottomless pit.

> Then I saw an angel coming down from heaven, having the key to the bottomless pit and a great chain in his hand. He laid hold of the dragon, that serpent of old, who is the Devil and Satan, and bound him for a thousand years; and he cast him into the bottomless pit, and shut him up, and set a seal on him, so that he should deceive the nations no more till the thousand years were finished. But after these things he must be released for a little while.
>
> —REVELATION 20:1–3

NATURE, PERSONALITY, AND CHARACTER OF DEMONS

They are evil.

> God sent a spirit of ill will between Abimelech and the men of Shechem; and the men of Shechem dealt treacherously with Abimelech.
>
> —JUDGES 9:23

They are intelligent.

> Now it happened, as we went to prayer, that a certain slave girl possessed with a spirit of divination met us, who brought her masters much profit by fortune-telling.
>
> —ACTS 16:16

They are powerful.

> Then they came to the other side of the sea, to the country of the Gadarenes. And when He had come out of the boat, immediately there met Him out of the tombs a man with an unclean spirit, who had his dwelling among the tombs; and no one could bind him, not even with chains, because he had often been bound with shackles and chains. And the chains had been pulled apart by him, and the shackles broken in pieces; neither could anyone tame him. And always, night and day, he was in the mountains and in the tombs, crying out and cutting himself with stones.
>
> —MARK 5:1–5

They have knowledge and understanding.

> And suddenly they cried out, saying, "What have we to do with You, Jesus, You Son of God? Have You come here to torment us before the time?"
>
> —MATTHEW 8:29; SEE ALSO LUKE 4:41; ACTS 19:15

They have emotions and sentiments.

> And he cried out with a loud voice and said, "What have I to do with You, Jesus, Son of the Most High God? I implore You by God that You do not torment me."
>
> —MARK 5:7

They have a table of communion.

Rather, that the things which the Gentiles sacrifice they sacrifice to demons and not to God, and I do not want you to have fellowship with demons. You cannot drink the cup of the Lord and the cup of demons; you cannot partake of the Lord's table and of the table of demons.

—1 CORINTHIANS 10:20–21

They have doctrines.

Now the Spirit expressly says that in latter times some will depart from the faith, giving heed to deceiving spirits and doctrines of demons.

—1 TIMOTHY 4:1

They have wills.

When an unclean spirit goes out of a man, he goes through dry places, seeking rest, and finds none. Then he says, "I will return to my house from which I came." And when he comes, he finds it empty, swept, and put in order. Then he goes and takes with him seven other spirits more wicked than himself, and they enter and dwell there; and the last state of that man is worse than the first. So shall it also be with this wicked generation.

—MATTHEW 12:43–45

They have miraculous powers.

> And I saw three unclean spirits like frogs coming out of the mouth of the dragon, out of the mouth of the beast, and out of the mouth of the false prophet. For they are spirits of demons, performing signs, which go out to the kings of the earth and of the whole world, to gather them to the battle of that great day of God Almighty.
>
> —Revelation 16:13–14

They have emotions.

> For unclean spirits, crying with a loud voice, came out of many who were possessed; and many who were paralyzed and lame were healed.
>
> —Acts 8:7

They have desires.

> When He had come to the other side, to the country of the Gergesenes, there met Him two demon-possessed men, coming out of the tombs, exceedingly fierce, so that no one could pass that way. And suddenly they cried out, saying, "What have we to do with You, Jesus, You Son of God? Have You come here to torment us before the time?" Now a good way off from them there was a herd of many swine feeding. So the demons begged Him, saying, "If You cast us out, permit us to go away into the herd of swine."
>
> —Matthew 8:28–31

They have a memory.

> And the evil spirit answered and said, "Jesus I know, and Paul I know; but who are you?"
>
> —ACTS 19:15

They have no body.

> And I saw three unclean spirits like frogs coming out of the mouth of the dragon, out of the mouth of the beast, and out of the mouth of the false prophet. For they are spirits of demons, performing signs, which go out to the kings of the earth and of the whole world, to gather them to the battle of that great day of God Almighty.
>
> —REVELATION 16:13–14

They are different from angels.

> For Sadducees say that there is no resurrection—and no angel or spirit; but the Pharisees confess both. Then there arose a loud outcry. And the scribes of the Pharisees' party arose and protested, saying, "We find no evil in this man; but if a spirit or an angel has spoken to him, let us not fight against God."
>
> —ACTS 23:8–9

Demons Worship and Are Worshipped

Idolatry is worship to the demons.

> They sacrificed to demons, not to God,
> To gods they did not know,
> To new gods, new arrivals
> That your fathers did not fear.
> —Deuteronomy 32:17

They have ministers that serve them.

> Therefore it is no great thing if his ministers also transform themselves into ministers of righteousness, whose end will be according to their works.
> —2 Corinthians 11:15

Sons of God can fall into the curse of serving other gods.

> So they left all the commandments of the Lord their God, made for themselves a molded image and two calves, made a wooden image and worshiped all the host of heaven, and served Baal. And they caused their sons and daughters to pass through the fire, practiced witchcraft and soothsaying, and sold themselves to do evil in the sight of the Lord, to provoke Him to anger.
> —2 Kings 17:16–17

79

The devil asked Christ to worship him.

Then the devil, taking Him up on a high mountain, showed Him all the kingdoms of the world in a moment of time. And the devil said to Him, "All this authority I will give You, and their glory; for this has been delivered to me, and I give it to whomever I wish. Therefore, if You will worship before me, all will be Yours."

—LUKE 4:5–7

Demonic cults have a table of communion.

Rather, that the things which the Gentiles sacrifice they sacrifice to demons and not to God, and I do not want you to have fellowship with demons. You cannot drink the cup of the Lord and the cup of demons; you cannot partake of the Lord's table and of the table of demons.

—1 CORINTHIANS 10:20–21

Demons are worshipped and offered sacrifices.

They shall no more offer their sacrifices to demons, after whom they have played the harlot. This shall be a statute forever for them throughout their generations.

—LEVITICUS 17:7

Men are condemned for worshipping demons.

But the rest of mankind, who were not killed by these plagues, did not repent of the works of their hands, that they should not worship demons, and idols of gold, silver, brass, stone, and wood, which can neither see nor hear nor walk. And they did not repent of their murders or their sorceries or their sexual immorality or their thefts.

—REVELATION 9:20–21

THE DIFFERENT SPIRITS THAT APPEAR IN THE BIBLE

The spirits of God and the spirits of Antichrist

Beloved, do not believe every spirit, but test the spirits, whether they are of God; because many false prophets have gone out into the world. By this you know the Spirit of God: Every spirit that confesses that Jesus Christ has come in the flesh is of God, and every spirit that does not confess that Jesus Christ has come in the flesh is not of God. And this is the spirit of the Antichrist, which you have heard was coming, and is now already in the world.

—1 JOHN 4:1–3

Deceiving spirits

Now the Spirit expressly says that in latter times some will depart from the faith, giving heed to deceiving spirits and doctrines of demons.

—1 TIMOTHY 4:1

Spirit of disobedience

> …in which you once walked according to the course of this world, according to the prince of the power of the air, the spirit who now works in the sons of disobedience.
>
> —EPHESIANS 2:2

Spirit of the world

> Now we have received, not the spirit of the world, but the Spirit who is from God, that we might know the things that have been freely given to us by God.
>
> —1 CORINTHIANS 2:12; SEE ALSO GALATIANS 1:4

Spirit of bondage

> For you did not receive the spirit of bondage again to fear, but you received the Spirit of adoption by whom we cry out, "Abba, Father."
>
> —ROMANS 8:15

Spirit of divination

> Now it happened, as we went to prayer, that a certain slave girl possessed with a spirit of divination met us, who brought her masters much profit by fortune-telling.
>
> —ACTS 16:16

Unclean spirit of idolatry

"It shall be in that day," says the LORD of hosts, "that I will cut off the names of the idols from the land, and they shall no longer be remembered. I will also cause the prophets and the unclean spirit to depart from the land."

—ZECHARIAH 13:2

Spirit of prostitution

Their deeds do not permit them
to return to their God.
A spirit of prostitution is in their heart;
they do not acknowledge the LORD.

—HOSEA 5:4, NIV; SEE ALSO HOSEA 4:12, NIV

Spirit of dizziness (confusion, bewilderment)

The LORD has poured into them a spirit of dizziness.

—ISAIAH 19:14, NIV

Spirit of sleep

For the LORD has poured out on you
The spirit of deep sleep.

—ISAIAH 29:10

Spirit of fear (fright)

> For God has not given us a spirit of fear, but of power and of love and of a sound mind.
>
> —2 Timothy 1:7; see also Job 4:15–16; Isaiah 21:4

Spirit of lies

> Then a spirit came forward and stood before the Lord, and said, "I will persuade him." The Lord said to him, "In what way?" So he said, "I will go out and be a lying spirit in the mouth of all his prophets." And the Lord said, "You shall persuade him, and also prevail. Go out and do so."
>
> —1 Kings 22:21–22

Evil spirit (ill will, animosity)

> Then the man in whom the evil spirit was leaped on them, overpowered them, and prevailed against them, so that they fled out of that house naked and wounded.
>
> —Acts 19:16; see also Judges 9:23

A haughty spirit (pride, arrogance)

> Pride goes before destruction,
> And a haughty spirit before a fall.
>
> —Proverbs 16:18

A broken spirit (sadness)

> A merry heart does good, like medicine,
> But a broken spirit dries the bones.
> —PROVERBS 17:22

Spirit of anger

> Do not hasten in your spirit to be angry,
> For anger rests in the bosom of fools.
> —ECCLESIASTES 7:9

Spirit of infirmity (sicknesses)

> And behold, there was a woman who had a spirit
> of infirmity eighteen years, and was bent over
> and could in no way raise herself up.
> —LUKE 13:11

The love of money

> But those who desire to be rich fall into temp-
> tation and a snare, and into many foolish and
> harmful lusts which drown men in destruction
> and perdition. For the love of money is a root
> of all kinds of evil, for which some have strayed
> from the faith in their greediness, and pierced
> themselves through with many sorrows.
> —1 TIMOTHY 6:9–10

Spirits that promote hypocrisy and lying

But a certain man named Ananias, with Sapphira his wife, sold a possession. And he kept back part of the proceeds, his wife also being aware of it, and brought a certain part and laid it at the apostles' feet. But Peter said, "Ananias, why has Satan filled your heart to lie to the Holy Spirit and keep back part of the price of the land for yourself? While it remained, was it not your own? And after it was sold, was it not in your own control? Why have you conceived this thing in your heart? You have not lied to men but to God."

—Acts 5:1–4

Spirits that sow doubt, mistrust, and ambition in man

And he [the serpent] said to the woman, "Has God indeed said, 'You shall not eat of every tree of the garden'?" And the woman said to the serpent, "We may eat the fruit of the trees of the garden; but of the fruit of the tree which is in the midst of the garden, God has said, 'You shall not eat it, nor shall you touch it, lest you die.'" Then the serpent said to the woman, "You will not surely die. For God knows that in the day you eat of it your eyes will be opened, and you will be like God, knowing good and evil." So when the woman saw that the tree was good for food, that it was pleasant to the eyes, and a tree desirable to make one wise, she took of its fruit

and ate. She also gave to her husband with her,
and he ate.

—GENESIS 3:1–6

Spirits that compel men to do diabolical and abominable damage

And I will come near you for judgment;
I will be a swift witness
Against sorcerers,
Against adulterers,
Against perjurers,
Against those who exploit wage earners and
    widows and orphans,
And against those who turn away an alien—
Because they do not fear Me,"
Says the LORD of hosts.

—MALACHI 3:5

Spirits who corrupt men to negotiate with the souls (through witchcraft, magic, charming, enchantment)

Thus says the Lord GOD: "Woe to the women
who sew magic charms on their sleeves and
make veils for the heads of people of every
height to hunt souls! Will you hunt the souls of
My people, and keep yourselves alive? And will
you profane Me among My people for handfuls
of barley and for pieces of bread, killing people
who should not die, and keeping people alive

who should not live, by your lying to My people
who listen to lies?"

—EZEKIEL 13:18–19

Spirits who deliver cities to the devil (sorceries)

Because of the multitude of harlotries of the
seductive harlot,
The mistress of sorceries,
Who sells nations through her harlotries,
And families through her sorceries.

—NAHUM 3:4

Spirits who put within Christians worldliness, indifference, and conformity

Do not love the world or the things in the world.
If anyone loves the world, the love of the Father
is not in him.

—1 JOHN 2:15

Spirits who cause sickness and poverty

Now a certain woman had a flow of blood for
twelve years, and had suffered many things from
many physicians. She had spent all that she had
and was no better, but rather grew worse.

—MARK 5:25–26

THE PURPOSES OF GOD TO PERMIT SATAN TO CONTINUE

To maintain man's humbleness

> And lest I should be exalted above measure by
> the abundance of the revelations, a thorn in the
> flesh was given to me, a messenger of Satan to
> buffet me, lest I be exalted above measure.
>
> —2 CORINTHIANS 12:7

To develop the character and faith of the believer

> Blessed is the man who endures temptation; for
> when he has been approved, he will receive the
> crown of life which the Lord has promised to
> those who love Him.
>
> —JAMES 1:12; SEE ALSO 1 PETER 1:7–13; 5:8–9;
> JUDE 20–24

To promote conflicts whereby the saints can be rewarded when they overcome

> You are of God, little children, and have over-
> come them, because He who is in you is greater
> than he who is in the world. They are of the
> world. Therefore they speak as of the world, and
> the world hears them. We are of God. He who
> knows God hears us; he who is not of God does
> not hear us. By this we know the spirit of truth
> and the spirit of error.
>
> —1 JOHN 4:4–6; SEE ALSO REVELATION 2:26–28

For destruction of the flesh so that the spirit may be saved

> In the name of our Lord Jesus Christ, when you are gathered together, along with my spirit, with the power of our Lord Jesus Christ, deliver such a one to Satan for the destruction of the flesh, that his spirit may be saved in the day of the Lord Jesus.
>
> —1 CORINTHIANS 5:4–5; SEE ALSO JOB 33:14–30;
> 2 CORINTHIANS 2:5–11

To demonstrate the power of God over all satanic power

> Then they were all amazed, so that they questioned among themselves, saying, "What is this? What new doctrine is this? For with authority He commands even the unclean spirits, and they obey Him."
>
> —MARK 1:27; SEE ALSO MARK 16:17–20;
> ACTS 13:6–10

To purify men and make them immune from all possibility of sinning in the eternal future

> Lest Satan should take advantage of us; for we are not ignorant of his devices.
>
> —2 CORINTHIANS 2:11

To perfect us in the knowledge of good and evil, of God and the devil, to encourage voluntary service to God

> Beloved, do not think it strange concerning the fiery trial which is to try you, as though some strange thing happened to you; but rejoice to the extent that you partake of Christ's sufferings, that when His glory is revealed, you may also be glad with exceeding joy. If you are reproached for the name of Christ, blessed are you, for the Spirit of glory and of God rests upon you. On their part He is blasphemed, but on your part He is glorified.
>
> —1 PETER 4:12–14; SEE ALSO HEBREWS 12:23

To permit the free will of man to be proven, being exposed to evil and thereby choosing the correct way to voluntarily decide to serve, believing in Christ as Lord and Savior

> Take my yoke upon you, and learn of me; for I am meek and lowly in heart: and ye shall find rest unto your souls.
>
> —MATTHEW 11:29, KJV; SEE ALSO
> DEUTERONOMY 11:26–28; 30:19

8

THE WORKS OF THE DEVIL

The reason the Son of God was made mani-
fest (visible) was to undo (destroy, loosen, and
dissolve) the works the devil [has done].

—1 John 3:8, AMP

WHEN WE UNDERSTAND the passages in chapter 7, we see that Satan attacks man by using a spirit. Many other adverse things that we may not understand could be attributed to the works of the devil. But Christ died to destroy and cancel all the works of the devil.

> …having wiped out the handwriting of require-
> ments that was against us, which was con-
> trary to us. And He has taken it out of the way,
> having nailed it to the cross. Having disarmed

principalities and powers, He made a public spectacle of them, triumphing over them in it.

—Colossians 2:14–15; see also Hebrews 2:14–15;
1 Peter 2:24; 1 John 3:8

And now every believer has been given authority over all the works of the enemy, as we see in Mark 16:17–20; John 14:12; and Revelation 12:7–11.

How Satan Works

Plans his cunning attacks against the home, man, and the church; instigates rebellion

Now the serpent was more cunning than any beast of the field which the Lord God had made. And he said to the woman, "Has God indeed said, 'You shall not eat of every tree of the garden'?" And the woman said to the serpent, "We may eat the fruit of the trees of the garden; but of the fruit of the tree which is in the midst of the garden, God has said, 'You shall not eat it, nor shall you touch it, lest you die.'" Then the serpent said to the woman, "You will not surely die. For God knows that in the day you eat of it your eyes will be opened, and you will be like God, knowing good and evil." So when the woman saw that the tree was good for food, that it was pleasant to the eyes, and a tree desirable to make one wise, she took of its fruit and ate. She also gave to her husband with her, and he ate.

—Genesis 3:1–6

But I fear, lest somehow, as the serpent deceived
Eve by his craftiness, so your minds may be corrupted from the simplicity that is in Christ.

—2 Corinthians 11:3

Promotes the works of darkness, including moral corruption and sexual perversion

And have no fellowship with the unfruitful
works of darkness, but rather expose them.

—Ephesians 5:11

Because, although they knew God, they did
not glorify Him as God, nor were thankful,
but became futile in their thoughts, and their
foolish hearts were darkened. Professing to be
wise, they became fools, and changed the glory
of the incorruptible God into an image made
like corruptible man—and birds and four-footed
animals and creeping things. Therefore God
also gave them up to uncleanness, in the lusts
of their hearts, to dishonor their bodies among
themselves, who exchanged the truth of God for
the lie, and worshiped and served the creature
rather than the Creator, who is blessed forever.
Amen.

—Romans 1:21–25; see also Jeremiah 2:19;
Acts 26:18; Ephesians 6:12

Works evil deeds, deaths, thefts, injustices, and the like

And even as they did not like to retain God in their knowledge, God gave them over to a debased mind, to do those things which are not fitting; being filled with all unrighteousness, sexual immorality, wickedness, covetousness, maliciousness; full of envy, murder, strife, deceit, evil-mindedness; they are whisperers, back-biters, haters of God, violent, proud, boasters, inventors of evil things, disobedient to parents, undiscerning, untrustworthy, unloving, unforgiving, unmerciful; who, knowing the righteous judgment of God, that those who practice such things are deserving of death, not only do the same but also approve of those who practice them.

—ROMANS 1:28–32; SEE ALSO COLOSSIANS 1:21

Causes spiritual blindness and lack of understanding

Whose minds the god of this age has blinded, who do not believe, lest the light of the gospel of the glory of Christ, who is the image of God, should shine on them.

—2 CORINTHIANS 4:4

Robs the Word of God from hearts (sleep, forgetfulness)

> When anyone hears the word of the kingdom, and does not understand it, then the wicked one comes and snatches away what was sown in his heart. This is he who received seed by the wayside.
>
> —MATTHEW 13:19

Deceives men with supernatural false works

> And no wonder! For Satan himself transforms himself into an angel of light.
>
> —2 CORINTHIANS 11:14

Accuses God's people

> Then I heard a loud voice saying in heaven, "Now salvation, and strength, and the kingdom of our God, and the power of His Christ have come, for the accuser of our brethren, who accused them before our God day and night, has been cast down."
>
> —REVELATION 12:10

Promotes and falsifies worship and miracles

> And then the lawless one will be revealed, whom the Lord will consume with the breath of His mouth and destroy with the brightness of His coming. The coming of the lawless one is according to the working of Satan, with all

power, signs, and lying wonders, and with all unrighteous deception among those who perish, because they did not receive the love of the truth, that they might be saved. And for this reason God will send them strong delusion, that they should believe the lie, that they all may be condemned who did not believe the truth but had pleasure in unrighteousness.

—2 Thessalonians 2:8–12

Causes storms and has power over the natural realm

While he was still speaking, another also came and said, "Your sons and daughters were eating and drinking wine in their oldest brother's house, and suddenly a great wind came from across the wilderness and struck the four corners of the house, and it fell on the young people, and they are dead; and I alone have escaped to tell you!"

—Job 1:18–19; see also Mark 4:35–41

Governs the nations

We know that we are of God, and the whole world lies under the sway of the wicked one.

—1 John 5:19; see also Matthew 4:8–10;
John 12:31

Had power over death and binds people with fear of dying

> Inasmuch then as the children have partaken of flesh and blood, He Himself likewise shared in the same, that through death He might destroy him who had the power of death, that is, the devil, and release those who through fear of death were all their lifetime subject to bondage.
>
> —HEBREWS 2:14–15

Hinders the growth of the gospel

> Therefore we wanted to come to you—even I, Paul, time and again—but Satan hindered us.
>
> —1 THESSALONIANS 2:18

Supervises the demons

> And war broke out in heaven: Michael and his angels fought with the dragon; and the dragon and his angels fought.
>
> —REVELATION 12:7

Causes incurable sickness

> And behold, there was a woman who had a spirit of infirmity eighteen years, and was bent over and could in no way raise herself up.
>
> —LUKE 13:11

Induces suicide

> Lord, have mercy on my son, for he is an epileptic and suffers severely; for he often falls into the fire and often into the water. So I brought him to Your disciples, but they could not cure him.
>
> —MATTHEW 17:15–16

Sows bad seed

> But while men slept, his enemy came and sowed tares among the wheat and went his way.
>
> —MATTHEW 13:25

Agitates the senses to make us disobey God

> But I fear, lest somehow, as the serpent deceived Eve by his craftiness, so your minds may be corrupted from the simplicity that is in Christ.
>
> —2 CORINTHIANS 11:3; SEE ALSO EPHESIANS 2:1–3

Always looking to devour Christians, especially those who love God

> Be sober, be vigilant; because your adversary the devil walks about like a roaring lion, seeking whom he may devour. Resist him, steadfast in the faith, knowing that the same sufferings are experienced by your brotherhood in the world.
>
> —1 PETER 5:8–9

Oppresses the people of God

> How God anointed Jesus of Nazareth with the
> Holy Spirit and with power, who went about
> doing good and healing all who were oppressed
> by the devil, for God was with Him.
>
> —ACTS 10:38; SEE ALSO PSALM 106:42

Tempts leaders with doubt, pride, and ambition

> Then Jesus, being filled with the Holy Spirit,
> returned from the Jordan and was led by the
> Spirit into the wilderness, being tempted for
> forty days by the devil.
>
> —LUKE 4:1–2; SEE ALSO HEBREWS 4:15

Sets a trap for us when we ignore his cunningness

> The proud have hidden a snare for me, and cords;
> They have spread a net by the wayside;
> They have set traps for me.
>
> —PSALM 140:5

Brings sexual temptations

> Do not deprive one another except with con-
> sent for a time, that you may give yourselves to
> fasting and prayer; and come together again so
> that Satan does not tempt you because of your
> lack of self-control.
>
> —1 CORINTHIANS 7:5

Through deep works

> Now to you I say, and to the rest in Thyatira, as
> many as do not have this doctrine, who have not
> known the depths of Satan, as they say, I will put
> on you no other burden.
>
> —REVELATION 2:24

Deceives men through the senses

> But I fear, lest somehow, as the serpent deceived
> Eve by his craftiness, so your minds may be cor-
> rupted from the simplicity that is in Christ.
>
> —2 CORINTHIANS 11:3

Tries to make friends with the believers

> And what accord has Christ with Belial? Or what
> part has a believer with an unbeliever?
>
> —2 CORINTHIANS 6:15

Can fill the heart of the believer to lie

> But Peter said, "Ananias, why has Satan filled
> your heart to lie to the Holy Spirit and keep back
> part of the price of the land for yourself?"
>
> —ACTS 5:3

Steals, kills, and destroys

> The thief does not come except to steal, and
> to kill, and to destroy. I have come that they

may have life, and that they may have it more abundantly.

—JOHN 10:10

Asks God permission to sift the saints

And the Lord said, "Simon, Simon! Indeed, Satan has asked for you, that he may sift you as wheat."

—LUKE 22:31

THE WORKS OF DEMONS

Cause unclean deaf and dumb spirits

As they went out, behold, they brought to Him a man, mute and demon-possessed. And when the demon was cast out, the mute spoke. And the multitudes marveled, saying, "It was never seen like this in Israel!"

—MATTHEW 9:32–33

When Jesus saw that the people came running together, He rebuked the unclean spirit, saying to it, "Deaf and dumb spirit, I command you, come out of him and enter him no more!"

—MARK 9:25

Cause blindness and dumbness

Then one was brought to Him who was demon-possessed, blind and mute; and He healed him, so that the blind and mute man both spoke and saw.

—MATTHEW 12:22

Cause severe suffering

A Canaanite woman from that vicinity came to him, crying out, "Lord, Son of David, have mercy on me! My daughter is suffering terribly from demon-possession."

—MATTHEW 15:22, NIV

Cause insanity and mania

Then they came to Jesus, and saw the one who had been demon-possessed and had the legion, sitting and clothed and in his right mind. And they were afraid.

—MARK 5:15; SEE ALSO MATTHEW 17:14–21

Involved in all forms of moral lewdness

Now the works of the flesh are evident, which are: adultery, fornication, uncleanness, lewdness...

—GALATIANS 5:19

Attack the nervous system

Then they brought him to Him. And when he saw Him, immediately the spirit convulsed him, and he fell on the ground and wallowed, foaming at the mouth.

—MARK 9:20

Can give a possessed man supernatural strength

Then they came to the other side of the sea, to the country of the Gadarenes. And when He had come out of the boat, immediately there met Him out of the tombs a man with an unclean spirit, who had his dwelling among the tombs; and no one could bind him, not even with chains, because he had often been bound with shackles and chains. And the chains had been pulled apart by him, and the shackles broken in pieces; neither could anyone tame him. And always, night and day, he was in the mountains and in the tombs, crying out and cutting himself with stones.

—MARK 5:1–5

Propagate and fabricate doctrines of demons

Now the Spirit expressly says that in latter times some will depart from the faith, giving heed to deceiving spirits and doctrines of demons.

—1 TIMOTHY 4:1

Cause lying

Then a spirit came forward and stood before the LORD, and said, "I will persuade him." The LORD said to him, "In what way?" So he said, "I will go out and be a lying spirit in the mouth of all his prophets." And the LORD said, "You shall persuade him, and also prevail. Go out and do so."

—1 KINGS 22:21–22

Cause love for the world and material things

> Do not love the world or the things in the world. If anyone loves the world, the love of the Father is not in him. For all that is in the world—the lust of the flesh, the lust of the eyes, and the pride of life—is not of the Father but is of the world. And the world is passing away, and the lust of it; but he who does the will of God abides forever.
>
> —1 JOHN 2:15–17

Cause strife and divisions

> For you are still carnal. For where there are envy, strife, and divisions among you, are you not carnal and behaving like mere men?
>
> —1 CORINTHIANS 3:3

Cause men to become violent

> A man shall eat well by the fruit of his mouth,
> But the soul of the unfaithful feeds on violence.
>
> —PROVERBS 13:2

Cause men to betray their friends

> And supper being ended, the devil having already put it into the heart of Judas Iscariot, Simon's son, to betray Him...
>
> —JOHN 13:2

Disturb prayer and delays the answer

> Then he said to me, "Do not fear, Daniel, for from the first day that you set your heart to understand, and to humble yourself before your God, your words were heard; and I have come because of your words. But the prince of the kingdom of Persia withstood me twenty-one days."
>
> —DANIEL 10:12–13

Manifest themselves through men or animals

> Now the serpent was more cunning than any beast of the field which the LORD God had made. And he said to the woman, "Has God indeed said, 'You shall not eat of every tree of the garden'?"
>
> —GENESIS 3:1; SEE ALSO MATTHEW 16:23

Resist being cast out

> And as he was still coming, the demon threw him down and convulsed him. Then Jesus rebuked the unclean spirit, healed the child, and gave him back to his father.
>
> —LUKE 9:42

Disturb and try to contaminate those who seek God

> Then they went into Capernaum, and immediately on the Sabbath He entered the synagogue and taught. And they were astonished at His teaching, for He taught them as one having authority, and not as the scribes. Now there was

a man in their synagogue with an unclean spirit. And he cried out, saying, "Let us alone! What have we to do with You, Jesus of Nazareth? Did You come to destroy us? I know who You are— the Holy One of God!" But Jesus rebuked him, saying, "Be quiet, and come out of him!" And when the unclean spirit had convulsed him and cried out with a loud voice, he came out of him. Then they were all amazed, so that they questioned among themselves, saying, "What is this? What new doctrine is this? For with authority He commands even the unclean spirits, and they obey Him."

—MARK 1:21–27

Believe and tremble

You believe that there is one God. You do well. Even the demons believe—and tremble!

—JAMES 2:19

Plan new and worse invasions

Then he goes and takes with him seven other spirits more wicked than himself, and they enter and dwell there; and the last state of that man is worse than the first. So shall it also be with this wicked generation.

—MATTHEW 12:45

Can enter into children; have no respect for age

So He asked his father, "How long has this been happening to him?" And he said, "From childhood."

—MARK 9:21; SEE ALSO MARK 7:25

Works abound

Also a multitude gathered from the surrounding cities to Jerusalem, bringing sick people and those who were tormented by unclean spirits, and they were all healed.

—ACTS 5:16; SEE ALSO ACTS 8:9; 19:19

Do not come out at the order of an unbeliever or heathen

Then some of the itinerant Jewish exorcists took it upon themselves to call the name of the Lord Jesus over those who had evil spirits, saying, "We exorcise you by the Jesus whom Paul preaches." Also there were seven sons of Sceva, a Jewish chief priest, who did so. And the evil spirit answered and said, "Jesus I know, and Paul I know; but who are you?" Then the man in whom the evil spirit was leaped on them, overpowered them, and prevailed against them, so that they fled out of that house naked and wounded.

—ACTS 19:13–16

Are not human and can be cast out

> And these signs will follow those who believe: In
> My name they will cast out demons.
>
> —MARK 16:17

**Devil is used as a title or name for Satan, the prince
of the demons.**

> But the Pharisees said, "He casts out demons by
> the ruler of the demons."
>
> —MATTHEW 9:34

**Satan is the highest diabolical leader and the source
of all evil in the universe.**

> The thief does not come except to steal, and
> to kill, and to destroy. I have come that they
> may have life, and that they may have it more
> abundantly.
>
> —JOHN 10:10

THE CAPACITIES OF DEMONS

The following list reveals some of the things demons can
do.

Teach

> Now the Spirit expressly says that in latter times
> some will depart from the faith, giving heed to
> deceiving spirits and doctrines of demons.
>
> —1 TIMOTHY 4:1

Rob

When anyone hears the word of the kingdom, and does not understand it, then the wicked one comes and snatches away what was sown in his heart. This is he who received seed by the wayside.

—MATTHEW 13:19; SEE ALSO LUKE 8:12; 1 PETER 5:8–9

Fight against Christians

For we do not wrestle against flesh and blood, but against principalities, against powers, against the rulers of the darkness of this age, against spiritual hosts of wickedness in the heavenly places.

—EPHESIANS 6:12

Get very angry

Therefore rejoice, O heavens, and you who dwell in them! Woe to the inhabitants of the earth and the sea! For the devil has come down to you, having great wrath, because he knows that he has a short time.

—REVELATION 12:12

Predict the future (divination)

Now it happened, as we went to prayer, that a certain slave girl possessed with a spirit of divination met us, who brought her masters much profit by fortune-telling.

—ACTS 16:16; SEE ALSO LEVITICUS 20:27

Familiarize themselves with evil men and form relationships with them

And the person who turns to mediums and familiar spirits, to prostitute himself with them, I will set My face against that person and cut him off from his people.

—LEVITICUS 20:6

Enter or come out of men until they are finally resisted

When an unclean spirit goes out of a man, he goes through dry places, seeking rest, and finds none. Then he says, "I will return to my house from which I came."

—MATTHEW 12:43–44; SEE ALSO MARK 9:25

Talk and imitate the dead

And when they say to you, "Seek those who are mediums and wizards, who whisper and mutter," should not a people seek their God? Should they seek the dead on behalf of the living?

—ISAIAH 8:19

Defend themselves

> And the evil spirit answered and said, "Jesus I know, and Paul I know; but who are you?" Then the man in whom the evil spirit was leaped on them, overpowered them, and prevailed against them, so that they fled out of that house naked and wounded.
>
> —ACTS 19:15–16

Reveal spiritual things

> Let us alone! What have we to do with You, Jesus of Nazareth? Did You come to destroy us? I know who You are—the Holy One of God!
>
> —MARK 1:24; SEE ALSO ACTS 16:16–18

Converse

> Now the serpent was more cunning than any beast of the field which the LORD God had made. And he said to the woman, "Has God indeed said, 'You shall not eat of every tree of the garden'?" And the woman said to the serpent, "We may eat the fruit of the trees of the garden; but of the fruit of the tree which is in the midst of the garden, God has said, 'You shall not eat it, nor shall you touch it, lest you die.'" Then the serpent said to the woman, "You will not surely die. For God knows that in the day you eat of it your eyes will be opened, and you will be like God, knowing good and evil."
>
> —GENESIS 3:1–5

SOME OF SATAN'S WORKS WILL NOT BE DESTROYED UNTIL THE END

The only works that will not be completely destroyed in these times are the following:

1. All sin and rebellion of man—Romans 1:27–31; 7:14–25

2. The government of Satan over the nations—1 John 5:19

3. The kingdom of death—Hebrews 9:27

4. The continued opposition of Satan toward the saints—Ephesians 6:12; 1 Peter 5:8

5. The existence of witchcraft and its works— Ezekiel 13:18–23; Galatians 5:19–21; Revelation 9:21; 21:8; 22:15

6. The existence of various religious and false works—Matthew 24:5, 11; 1 Timothy 4:1; 2 Peter 2:1

7. The fierceness of animals and their attacks on man—Ecclesiastes 10:8

Nevertheless, all these works will be destroyed forever in the millennium.

Then comes the end, when He delivers the kingdom to God the Father, when He puts an end to all rule and all authority and power. For He must reign till He has put all enemies under His feet. The last enemy that will be destroyed is death. For "He has put all things under His feet." But when He says "all things are put under Him," it is evident that He who put all things under Him is excepted. Now when all things are made subject to Him, then the Son Himself will also be subject to Him who put all things under Him, that God may be all in all.

—1 CORINTHIANS 15:24–28

The Ministry of Deliverance

9

THE DELIVERANCE MINISTRY

My people are destroyed for lack of knowledge.
—Hosea 4:6

THE GREATEST CHALLENGE for a believer who needs
and desires deliverance is seeking knowledge about
his spiritual nature and condition and how sin
affects every area of his life. Deliverance without educa-
tion can attain only temporary effectiveness. We must
lead and instruct the believer to understand his spiritual
and emotional crisis before attempting the deliverance
process. Only then will the process be effective.

MEANING OF DELIVERANCE

Deliverance can mean, "release from captivity, slavery,
oppression, or any restraint; rescue from danger or any
evil." "God sent me…to save your lives by a great deliverance" (Gen. 45:7, NIV). It also can mean, "setting at

liberty, canceling a debt, salvation, taking out, preservation from, rescue, relief, escape, and freedom."

The desire of the person needing to be set free and seeking deliverance should be to surrender voluntarily to the Lordship of Jesus Christ. His soul, mind, body, and spirit must be involved.

To be set free means that the person chooses to replace his values and personal desires for those of the kingdom of God. The person has reached the place where he is now ready to be cleansed of all impurities and iniquities.

> That you put off, concerning your former conduct, the old man which grows corrupt according to the deceitful lusts, and be renewed in the spirit of your mind, and that you put on the new man which was created according to God, in true righteousness and holiness.
> —EPHESIANS 4:22–24

The church is called to fulfill the Great Commission of making disciples, teaching them, healing the sick, and setting the captives free. The same Spirit that was operating in Jesus's deliverance ministry on earth also dwells in every believer.

> The Spirit of the LORD is upon Me,
> Because He has anointed Me
> To preach the gospel to the poor;
> He has sent Me to heal the brokenhearted,
> To proclaim liberty to the captives

And recovery of sight to the blind,
To set at liberty those who are oppressed.

—LUKE 4:18

If we compare the deliverance ministry of today with the way Jesus did it, we will find some interesting facts.

Public exorcism was a part of Jesus's normal, daily ministry. Although the people of that day recognized and practiced exorcism, Jesus cast out demons with an authority that amazed the people.

The major miracles of Jesus's ministry, such as healing, controlling nature, and raising the dead, had all occurred through one or more of the Old Testament prophets. But the casting out of demons was unique to Jesus, and it revealed that the authority of the kingdom of God was present. Most of the people whom Jesus cast demons out of were normal and decent religious Jews.

If demons were a problem in the synagogues of orthodox Israel, why would they be a lesser problem in the churches of modern America?

Demons have two assignments:

1. They are to keep mankind from knowing Jesus Christ as Savior and Lord.

2. If they fail at that, they are to keep believers from serving Jesus Christ effectively.

TWO PRIMARY SOURCES OF HUMAN PROBLEMS

As we stated in the Introduction to this book, there are two primary sources of human problems: *the flesh* and *demons*. We cannot cast out the flesh, as much as we might like to. Neither can we crucify the demons.

Demon activity in general will keep a person from permanent victory. Temporary relief can be attained by spending time in Bible study, prayer, and fasting or by practicing discipline, but the problem will recur, bringing defeat and discouragement. A demon watches for a moment of weakness and then attacks the person in a particular area.

Compulsive behavior may be demonic. If a person confesses and repents repeatedly of a certain sin but cannot seem to get a release, he could be a slave to demon power.

Demons will make a person feel dirty and unclean. They often inject vile thoughts and images into the mind, especially when the person is seeking to study God's Word or serve God and His people.

> If there is sin between a person and God, deliverance will not come until the sin is confessed.

An example of one sin that holds back many women from deliverance is deliberate abortion. God will forgive it, but it must be confessed as murder.

When the Spirit of God abides in a person, He will not allow the works of the enemy to stay hidden. As the Spirit of God reveals the works of the enemy, the believer must arise and gird himself with faith and resist the enemy in every area until he is free to be all God wants him to be. There is no substitute for repentance, self-discipline, the crucifixion of the flesh, or forgiveness and confession of faults.

Here are some basic things to look for in a person who wants to be set free:

1. Discern if the person's will is active or not.

2. Ask if the person is unable to cope with everyday problems.

3. See if there are many unfinished jobs or projects.

4. Determine if the person has lack of concentration.

5. Observe if the person exhibits *mechanical* motions.

6. Discern if the person is unable to make decisions or to initiate actions.

If the person ceases to be active, God cannot use him because his will is no longer in action. Evil spirits take easy advantage of passivity. Passivity assumes that God is deciding everything for that person.

From the LORD comes deliverance. May your
blessing be on your people.

—PSALM 3:8, NIV

10

QUALIFICATIONS FOR THE DELIVERANCE MINISTRY

The Spirit of the Lord is upon Me, because He has anointed Me to preach the gospel to the poor; He has sent Me to heal the brokenhearted, to proclaim liberty to the captives and recovery of sight to the blind, to set at liberty those who are oppressed.

—LUKE 4:18

THE MINISTRY OF deliverance is given to the body of Christ to be used with the principal ministries of the church. I believe there is a special anointing given to different individuals through whom the gifts of discernment operate, and these believers are able to minister to people who are oppressed of the devil.

This ministry demands preparation and loyalty to God. Prayer support is necessary to enter into battle against spiritual forces to bring deliverance. The person's personal life must be a life of discipline in prayer, fasting, and the Word.

Purity in your personal life is a must. The believer who is free to move unmolested into enemy territory is the one who has a passion for righteousness and a hatred for evil. He must be clean of all defilement of flesh and spirit, perfecting holiness in the fear of the Lord.

The deliverance minister must be in control of the time he gives to his ministry. Do not allow the devil to push you into ministry. You must call the terms and be in control. The minister must limit the hours and days to be given to the ministry.

REQUIREMENTS BEFORE ADMINISTERING DELIVERANCE

Several questions must be asked prior to ministering deliverance.

1. Is the person ready or just wanting temporary relief?

2. Does the person want only temporary ministry, not permanent deliverance?

3. Does the person have enough truth to maintain deliverance?

Pray for discernment. Discernment is a gift and is developed by experience and alertness.

Pray for power and authority. Power comes from the Holy Spirit according to your degree of faith. If you experience victory in your own individual life, then God's power in your life is evident.

> Submission to authority gives authority. The fullness of the Holy Spirit gives power.

Satan is the father of lies and deception. We must confront the lies of Satan with the Word of God. The Word gives us the power and authority. It is a two-edged sword.

- God is our strength (Ps. 18:1–3).

- He gives ministry to those who have clean hands (Ps. 18:20–24).

- He gives us supernatural strength (Ps. 18:32–36).

- He is our protection (Isa. 41:10–13).

REQUIREMENTS FOR A DELIVERANCE MINISTER

In order to be an effective deliverance minister, a believer must be grounded in the Word. He must know what the Word has to say about Satan and his demons, their power, and their weaknesses.

He must act according to the Word of God and not according to man's knowledge from past experiences.

He must know his authority and act on it in faith, believing with a fearless approach. He must show no signs of fear. He must also be immune to the critical spirits of men and women.

He must always walk in the strength of the Lord under the direction of the Holy Spirit.

He cannot show any signs of physical illness, fear, emotional distress, or defeat.

In other words, it takes guts to live a victorious life daily as a minister of deliverance.

REWARDS OF THE OVERCOMER

Here are just some of the rewards God gives to His overcomers:

> For whatever is born of God overcomes the world.
>
> —1 JOHN 5:4

> These things I have spoken to you, that in Me you may have peace. In the world you will have tribulation; but be of good cheer, I have overcome the world.
>
> —JOHN 16:33

> Be not overcome of evil, but overcome evil with good.
>
> —ROMANS 12:21, KJV

> To him who overcomes I will give to eat from the tree of life, which is in the midst of the Paradise of God.
>
> —REVELATION 2:7

He who overcomes shall not be hurt by the second death.

—REVELATION 2:11

To him who overcomes I will give some of the hidden manna to eat.

—REVELATION 2:17

He who overcomes shall be clothed in white garments, and I will not blot out his name from the Book of Life; but I will confess his name before My Father and before His angels.

—REVELATION 3:5

To him who overcomes I will grant to sit with Me on My throne, as I also overcame and sat down with My Father on His throne.

—REVELATION 3:21–22

EVIL SPIRITS AND RELATED MANIFESTATIONS

Below is a list of some evil spirits with their related manifestations.

1. Rejection—fear of rejection, self-rejection, rebellion

2. Lust—sexual or worldly

3. Accusation—self-accusation, accusation of others, negative confessions

4. Self-will—selfishness, stubbornness

5. Self-delusion—self-deception

6. Jealousy—envy, suspicion, distrust, persecution, confrontation

7. Memory recall—resentment, unforgiveness, mind binding, mind control, melancholy, loneliness, sadness

8. Addictive spirits—alcohol, drugs, tobacco, gluttony, cravings, desire

9. Financial lack—poverty

10. Self-pity—false compassion, false responsibility

11. Bitterness—hatred, anger, violence, suicide, murder, death, retaliation

12. Perfection—pride, vanity, ego, frustration, intolerance

13. Judgmental—critical, fear of judgment, unteachable

14. Guilt—unworthiness, shame

15. Depression—hopelessness, discouragement, despondency, despair

16. Infirm spirits—headaches, rheumatism, arthritis, diabetes, blood impurities,

cancers, tumors, heart trouble, blindness, deafness, allergies

17. Tired and lazy spirits—doubt, unbelief, lying, procrastination

18. Self-awareness—timidity, shyness, sensitiveness, talkativeness

19. Fantasy—unfairness, daydreaming, unreality, vivid imagination, pouting, withdrawal

20. Nervousness—tensions, fears, mental insanity

21. Witchcraft—cults, occult, curses, darkness, antichrist, control, possessiveness

22. Religious spirits—familiar spirits, schizophrenia, confusion

Deliverance Prayer

Repeat this prayer under the direction of a deliverance minister:

Heavenly Father, I come before You now with joy in my heart, believing that You are going to set me free from all demonic hindrances in my life and in my walk with You. I confess all of my sins to You, Father, especially the sins of resentment and unforgiveness against others.

I also confess all the sins I have committed in my entire lifetime and those I failed to confess and have forgotten about. I accept Your forgiveness, and I repent for having all these things in my heart.

Father, when I am free, I confess that I will no longer rule and reign in my own life. I will allow the Holy Spirit to direct my life from this moment forward, day by day. Now I am going back to the cross to crucify my flesh with Jesus. Father, I am laying all of my problems, large and small, at the foot of the cross. I am leaving them there for You to handle, Father, and I thank You in advance for doing this for me.

I am leaving the cross now under the direction of the Holy Spirit, and I expect the perfect plan for my life to unfold. I also expect Your help to minister with signs, wonders, and miracles to glorify Your name.

I now declare, Satan, by the authority invested in me by Jesus Christ at Calvary, I come against you and all your demons in my life! [Renounce all the spirits of the flesh listed in God's Word, as well as all inherited spirits and the spirits related to them. Renounce any demons that are a factor in your life, plus anything else that might hinder your family life, whether it has been named or not, inherited or otherwise. Then, with the direction of your deliverance minister, cast all these things out of your life by using your own spiritual authority. Send these things to the dry places forever.] Amen.

11

How to Keep Your Freedom

*And whoever shall call on the name of the
Lord shall be delivered and saved.*

—Joel 2:32, AMP

MANY TIMES BELIEVERS who have been taken
through deliverance by a deliverance minister,
and have been totally delivered from evil influ-
ences and demonic oppression, seem to have the same
problems or worse a short time later. This causes a great
deal of confusion and lack of belief in the credibility of
the deliverance ministry. *It is the intent of this teaching
to clear up confusion and bring scriptural light on how
to keep one's deliverance.*

Deliverance from demonic oppression is not a *quick
fix* or *magic pill* to help someone be free from problems.
The person delivered must play an active part in maintaining the freedom the Lord has manifested in his or
her life.

Sometimes the problems that arise after deliverance are the result of exuberance. Some people are so excited after going through deliverance that they forget the instructions given on how to remain free. Sometimes the problems are a result of ignorance of God's instructions about the requirements for deliverance and what the Scriptures say regarding failures in our lives.

We need to remember that a person who needs deliverance has been injured deeply by Satan and may have a hard time living a normal life. He has been weakened morally, physically, and spiritually. Although the power of the enemy over his life has been broken after deliverance, he will sometimes need spiritual support until strong enough to resist Satan on his own. This does not mean we need to constantly baby him, but rather bring spiritual instruction from Scripture and be a prayer support for him.

As a newly saved person needs guidance and support, so does a newly delivered person. Too many are left to wander in a wilderness of defeat and conflict because of a lack of spiritual help after deliverance. *Teaching is necessary for defense against future satanic onslaughts so that the person can obtain a total victory.*

Weakened minds need to be transformed to the mind of Christ.

This takes time and help from other Christians, especially in the cases of those who have been freed from witchcraft, curses, or satanic worship. They must learn to walk with God and be strengthened and built up in the Word and in holy faith.

There are positive steps that Christians must take in order to continue walking in the newfound freedom of deliverance. Deliverance is a wonderful experience that God wants us to walk in every day. His Word teaches it. As already stated, it is the intent of this teaching to bring God's Word to light so that many can live victoriously through Jesus Christ.

Twelve Steps to Maintaining Your Freedom

1. Do not discuss your deliverance with those who do not believe in this type of ministry.

> Do not give what is holy to the dogs; nor cast your pearls before swine, lest they trample them under their feet, and turn and tear you in pieces.
> —MATTHEW 7:6

An unbeliever will almost always give you his view on the subject of deliverance. When you asked the Lord Jesus to save you, you believed by faith that He did. Take your deliverance the same way, and don't listen to negative talk about it.

A person who does not believe in the deliverance ministry probably does not believe in demons. Satan will use that person to try to turn your mind again. As soon as you doubt, you open the door for oppression once again, and it's usually much greater oppression than before.

> Now He could do no mighty work there, except
> that He laid His hands on a few sick people and
> healed them. And He marveled because of their
> unbelief.
>
> —Mark 6:5–6

If you received your deliverance with faith and expectation, you were probably excited and wanted to tell someone right away. It doesn't mean that if there was no outward emotion there was no deliverance.

There may be people with whom you share your deliverance testimony who will doubt and not receive your ministry. You will marvel at their unbelief, but plant the seed and move on. There are other places to go and other people to teach. The key is to marvel at their unbelief yet continue believing God's Word to deliver and set captives free.

The Word says that whosoever shall call on the name of the Lord shall be delivered (Joel 2:32). You called on the Lord when seeking deliverance, now believe He will do what He says He will do. "God is not a man, that He should lie" (Num. 23:19).

Again, the key is to *believe*. God commands us to seek Him diligently. Our relationship with our Lord depends on our believing and obeying His commandments. The enemy would have you stop believing so you will stop obeying.

No one can tear down your belief unless you allow it.

As you believe, you close the door to Satan and open your heart to the Holy Spirit and allow Him to work in your life. The Lord said the battle is His, and we should rejoice that God wants to do battle for us. Stay away from the unbeliever Satan would use against you until you become grounded in your healing and deliverance. Allow God to build you up in your new level of faith.

2. Destroy all occult objects and literature.

Be careful what you bring into your home. Read only those things pleasing to God.

> And many who had believed came confessing and telling their deeds. Also, many of those who had practiced magic brought their books together and burned them in the sight of all. And they counted up the value of them, and it totaled fifty thousand pieces of silver.
>
> —ACTS 19:18–19

The Word says, "Submit to God. Resist the devil and He will flee from you" (James 4:7). Ask God to convict you of things in your home that are displeasing to Him. He will reveal them to you. Throw away or destroy anything satanic, such as Ouija boards, occult books and games, pentagrams, tarot cards, statues, idols, and the like. Don't allow anything pornographic in your home. There is a treacherous and perverse spirit connected with pornography. Don't give the devil an inch. Don't leave any door open for him to oppress you again.

> When you come into the land which the LORD your God is giving you, you shall not learn to follow the abominations of those nations. There shall not be found among you anyone who makes his son or his daughter pass through the fire, or one who practices witchcraft, or a soothsayer, or one who interprets omens, or a sorcerer, or one who conjures spells, or a medium, or a spiritist, or one who calls up the dead. For all who do these things are an abomination to the LORD, and because of these abominations the LORD your God drives them out from before you. You shall be blameless before the LORD your God.
>
> —DEUTERONOMY 18:9–13

You must have nothing to do with the land the Lord has delivered you from. Shun all appearance of evil. The Lord said in verse 13, "Be blameless." This means to be sincere and upright. Be sincere with the Lord and be upright by coming away from satanic slavery, and allow God to keep you walking in freedom.

3. Study the Scriptures daily and spend time apart with God.

Become a doer of the Word and not only a hearer.

> Be diligent to present yourself approved to God,
> a worker who does not need to be ashamed,
> rightly dividing the word of truth.
>
> —2 Timothy 2:15

It is important to know Scripture so that you can speak forth the Word when the enemy tries to deceive you. You will be a worker who does not need to be ashamed because the Lord can work quickly when His Word is spoken forth. His Word will never return void, but it will accomplish what pleases Him (Isa. 55:11).

Reading the Word every day keeps your mind sharp and keeps you built up in the faith. The enemy tries to destroy your faith all the time. Faith comes by hearing the Word of God.

> So then faith comes by hearing, and hearing by
> the word of God.
>
> —Romans 10:17

> It is written, "Man shall not live by bread alone,
> but by every word that proceeds from the mouth
> of God."
>
> —Matthew 4:4

The Word is food to your spirit just as bread is food to your body. If you don't stay in the Word, your spirit will be undernourished. This allows the enemy a window of possible entry. He is always looking for a way back into the house he was ejected from.

141

As newborn babes, desire the sincere milk of the
word, that ye may grow thereby.

—1 Peter 2:2, kjv

Don't be of the attitude that you have heard the Word
over and over and it is only milk to you. There is power
in every letter of the Word. Ask the Lord to give you new
revelation every time you read the Word. Ask the Lord to
give you a desire to receive the Word as a newborn babe.
Desire makes a big difference in how you grow spiritually.

Your word is a lamp to my feet
And a light to my path.

—Psalm 119:105

Allow God to guide you home, to be your light along
the journey He has set before you. Make good confessions, speak forth the Word of God, and let Him work
in your life.

This Book of the Law shall not depart from your
mouth, but you shall meditate in it day and night,
that you may observe to do according to all that
is written in it. For then you will make your way
prosperous, and then you will have good success.

—Joshua 1:8

If you meditate and follow the Word, allowing your
mind to always be conscious of obeying the Word, God
says you will prosper and have good success. On the
other hand, if you do not study and obey God's Word,

how can you expect to succeed and prosper? Sometimes a little humbling from the Lord will be necessary. Do not despise the discipline, but be grateful because His discipline keeps you clean. (See Hebrews 12:5–6.)

We have to respond to the Word of God and allow it to change our lives instead of trying to change the Word to fit our lifestyle.

> Be angry, and do not sin.
> Meditate within your heart on your bed, and be
>   still.
> —Psalm 4:4

We must maintain a healthy fear of the Lord if our lives are to remain in balance. As we commune with God and meditate upon His Word, God will commune with us. It is impossible for our enemies to oppress us if we maintain a pure relationship with God.

> My son, give attention to my words;
> Incline your ear to my sayings.
> Do not let them depart from your eyes;
> Keep them in the midst of your heart;
> For they are life to those who find them,
> And health to all their flesh.
> Keep your heart with all diligence,
> For out of it spring the issues of life.
> —Proverbs 4:20–23

Reading the Word will bring life to the spirit man and health to the physical man. We are commanded to keep our heart pure by staying in the Word of God.

> Brood of vipers! How can you, being evil, speak good things? For out of the abundance of the heart the mouth speaks. A good man out of the good treasure of his heart brings forth good things, and an evil man out of the evil treasure brings forth evil things.
>
> —Matthew 12:34–35

When God's Word is rooted and grounded in your Spirit, it will enable you to discern what is evil and what is good, what is pleasing to God and displeasing to God. You will then be able to see and stay on the path God has for your life and avoid pitfalls and the need for further deliverance sessions.

> But be doers of the word, and not hearers only, deceiving yourselves. For if anyone is a hearer of the word and not a doer, he is like a man observing his natural face in a mirror; for he observes himself, goes away, and immediately forgets what kind of man he was. But he who looks into the perfect law of liberty and continues in it, and is not a forgetful hearer but a doer of the work, this one will be blessed in what he does.
>
> —James 1:22–25

There is a powerful source of wisdom and strength available to you from God's Word. If you don't obey and do what the Word commands, you are deceiving yourself. To be able to hear and understand the Word, it must be read and meditated upon repeatedly until you hear what it says deep down in your heart. As the Word is renewed constantly in your mind and it gets into your heart, it will become engrafted in your spirit. The engrafted word will become your source of all good things. It will become an anchor in times of tribulations. After you hear the Word, God expects you to act upon it. If you do not put the Word into action, you will soon forget it. As an example, the more you do a task at home or work, the easier it becomes because of constant repetition. It is the same with God's Word. The more I say, "Lord, forgive me as I forgive others," the more I make sure I am always ready to forgive others. This practice will enable you to become a doer of God's Word. God will then bless you by helping you with your burdens and your infirmities. God has provided all you need in His Word, including how to keep your deliverance and how to use your authority over all the works of the enemy.

> For it is not those who hear the law who are righteous in God's sight, but it is those who obey the law who will be declared righteous.
>
> —ROMANS 2:13, NIV

This scripture commands us again to be doers. Many go to church services to hear, read, and gain knowledge of the Bible. But God is looking for doers. We have been put upon this earth to be doers, helpers, and ministers, people who care about the kingdom of God.

Jesus and His words are our example. But until we find God's direction for our lives, how can we do what He gave us authority to do? We must have the kind of faith Jesus had in God. Then we will be able to fulfill the plan God has for our lives. We may have a general direction, but God has a perfect direction for us.

4. Develop a consistent prayer life.

Pray in the spirit many times daily. Commune frequently with God.

> For if I pray in a tongue, my spirit prays, but my mind is unfruitful. So what shall I do? I will pray with my spirit, but I will also pray with my mind; I will sing with my spirit, but I will also sing with my mind.
>
> —1 CORINTHIANS 14:14–15, NIV

Paul believed in praying and singing in tongues and with understanding (his mind). He spoke in tongues more than all the Corinthian church. Many times you will not know what to pray for or how to pray over a specific situation. As you pray in tongues, the Holy Spirit will make intercession for you according to the will of God (Rom. 8:26–27).

Why do we sing in the spirit and with our understanding? Singing is praise unto the Lord, and the Lord inhabits the praises of His people (Ps. 22:3). We enter into a different dimension every time we praise and sing unto the Lord. The Holy Spirit participates with us in our praise. Singing and praising take us away from the worldly problems and trials and into the presence of the Holy Spirit, where all blessings proceed from.

> But you, dear friends, building yourselves up on
> your most holy faith, praying in the Holy Spirit.
> —JUDE 20

You cannot stay on your knees twenty-four hours a day, but you can stay in an attitude of prayer by keeping in touch with the Lord all day. You do this by speaking to yourself in psalms, hymns, and spiritual songs, singing and making melody in your hearts to the Lord (Eph. 5:19). As you do this, you are always communing with God, ready to pray at a moment's notice for any situation. God needs people willing to pray.

> And pray in the Spirit on all occasions with all
> kinds of prayers and requests. With this in mind,
> be alert and always keep on praying for all the
> saints.
> —EPHESIANS 6:18, NIV

Satan's most powerful weapon in this day is to attack your mind.

If he can keep you confused and withdrawn, he can do great damage. A word of caution—as Satan attacks the mind, many times he'll introduce spiritual pride to keep you withdrawn to yourself. You need to overcome pride and confess your faults to each other, and also pray one for another. As you confess your faults one to another, you are submitting to God, and you have the promise that the devil will flee from you.

Important: don't go around confessing to just anyone. You must be spiritually in tune with someone you trust to keep your confession between that person and God. No one else needs to know. Ask God for divine wisdom.

5. Have spiritual fellowship with other believers.

> But if we walk in the light as He is in the light, we have fellowship with one another, and the blood of Jesus Christ His Son cleanses us from all sin.
>
> —1 JOHN 1:7

Fellowship with other believers offers to you the privilege of experiencing the different gifts of the Spirit available to the body of Christ (1 Cor. 12:7–14).

> Not forsaking the assembling of ourselves together, as is the manner of some, but exhorting one another, and so much the more as you see the Day approaching.
>
> —HEBREWS 10:25

The Lord commands us to assemble together because He knows we cannot make it on our own. We are vulnerable to attack when we remain alone for too long. There is strength in numbers. One will put a thousand to flight, and two will put ten thousand to flight (Deut. 32:30).

There is great encouragement when we unite together with other believers to receive teaching and fellowship with one another

6. Guard your mind and thoughts. Refuse to think negative, critical, resentful, or selfish thoughts.

> Be anxious for nothing, but in everything by prayer and supplication, with thanksgiving, let your requests be made known to God; and the peace of God, which surpasses all understanding, will guard your hearts and minds through Christ Jesus.
>
> —PHILIPPIANS 4:6–7

Be careful for nothing. The Lord wants to do battle for us and give us peace. He promises to bring peace, which passes all understanding as we bring everything to Him in prayer. If you allow your mind to think negative thoughts, you cannot be at peace. God is not negative, nor can He abide with negativity.

These are the thoughts God can abide with:

> Finally, brethren, whatever things are true, whatever things are noble, whatever things are just, whatever things are pure, whatever things

are lovely, whatever things are of good report,
if there is any virtue and if there is anything
praiseworthy—meditate on these things.

—PHILIPPIANS 4:8

He commands us to train our mind in this positive
direction.

You will keep him in perfect peace,
Whose mind is stayed on You,
Because he trusts in You.

—ISAIAH 26:3

You are snared by the words of your mouth;
You are taken by the words of your mouth.

—PROVERBS 6:2

All the thoughts you continuously entertain will
become reality by the words you speak.

Your words are very powerful because you act upon
the words you speak. Negative thoughts that enter will
be negative words that will come out of your mouth.
When you speak negatively, your spirit is weakened and
the enemy has an open door.

**7. Use your God-given authority in the name of Jesus
to bind, loose, rebuke, and cast out demonic and evil
powers.**

And when He got into the boat, he who had been
demon-possessed begged Him that he might be

with Him. However, Jesus did not permit him, but said to him, "Go home to your friends, and tell them what great things the Lord has done for you, and how He has had compassion on you." And he departed and began to proclaim in Decapolis all that Jesus had done for him; and all marveled.

—MARK 5:18–20

The intent of this teaching is also to help new believers who go through the process of deliverance to build up their faith so that they learn to depend on God and resist any returning demons. It is necessary, however, that every person learn to depend on the Holy Spirit for himself and not to cling to other people every time they face a problem. The natural tendency for people who have just gone through deliverance is to depend on the person who helped them receive deliverance. It may be dangerous to the spiritual welfare of the person. Jesus did not permit the Gaderene to stay with Him after he was set free, although the man pleaded with Jesus to do so.

Demons go through dry places seeking rest. Why can't we cast them into the pit? It is because the Lord did not give us those instructions. Jesus reserves the right to condemn Satan and his demons in the end time. We have the authority in the name of Jesus Christ to bind and cast out demons into the dry and uninhabited places. "When an unclean spirit goes out of a man, he goes through dry places, seeking rest; and finding none, he says, 'I will return to my house from which I came'" (Luke 11:24; see also Matt. 12:43).

8. Confess your deliverance by faith, not by your feelings.

> And it shall come to pass
> That whoever calls on the name of the LORD
> Shall be saved.
> For in Mount Zion and in Jerusalem there shall
> be deliverance.
>
> —JOEL 2:32

Strong's Concordance defines *deliverance* in this context as "to escape." We can also define *deliverance* as "an escaped portion." That is what we are, a portion that has been set free to be all that the Lord wants us to be and to remain free. You need to be able to discern when the enemy is mounting an attack. It is very important to surround yourself with like-minded people. There is great power in numbers. Covenant with one another. Pray for one another. Confess your faults one to another and get the victory in Jesus. Hallelujah!

> I am your portion and your inheritance among
> the children of Israel.
>
> —NUMBERS 18:20

Having faith in what the Lord has done for us is to believe and have assurance of something. We must be very careful in our belief and follow the admonition in

Hebrews 3:12: "Beware, brethren, lest there be in any of you an evil heart of unbelief in departing from the living God."

If you are having trouble believing, talk to the Lord about it. He will help! Don't be afraid to pray, "Lord, I believe; help my unbelief!" God knows everything. We just need to cooperate.

The faith walk is sometimes a hard walk because of so many distractions in a sensual world. The Word says:

> For we do not wrestle against flesh and blood, but against principalities, against powers, against the rulers of the darkness of this age, against spiritual hosts of wickedness in the heavenly places.
>
> —EPHESIANS 6:12

The enemy is not going to sit idly by and say nothing about your deliverance. He will throw all sorts of obstacles in your path, probably daily. You must walk by what the Word tells you and not by how circumstances seem around you. Just remember that the enemy will do anything to get you back so that he can kill you, just as he is going to die. When he lies to you, tell him to get behind you in the name of Jesus. Spiritually the enemy is under your feet.

> But without faith it is impossible to please Him, for he who comes to God must believe that He

is, and that He is a rewarder of those who diligently seek Him.

—HEBREWS 11:6

So many times in the Old Testament Israel fell away from God, and it grieved Him. I believe God sheds tears when we don't believe Him. Let us also remember that some of the fathers could not enter into the Lord's rest because of unbelief. The Greek rendering for "rest" is the *repose* of Christianity—as a type of heaven.

We must believe that God is a rewarder of those who diligently seek Him. Take your eyes off the world. Sometimes it seems like the carnal person is reaping all the rewards. But remember, for those who don't come to Jesus, their rewards on earth are all they will have. We have eternal life with Jesus. Anything He rewards us with here on earth is an added blessing. Let us keep our eyes on what is most important.

> Now this is the confidence that we have in Him, that if we ask anything according to His will, He hears us. And if we know that He hears us, whatever we ask, we know that we have the petitions that we have asked of Him.
>
> —1 JOHN 5:14–15

When you asked the Lord to save you, you had to accept it by faith that He did. Even though we believe the Lord for salvation, many times we have trouble believing Him for anything else.

This scripture says, "If we ask anything according to His will…" Is it God's will for us to live with demonic oppression? Of course not! He said to resist the devil. Just as Satan came to tell you that you were not really saved, he will come to tell you that you are not really delivered of demonic oppression.

Satan will even try to convince you that there is no such thing as demons. The Word tells us we don't have to listen to Satan's lies. When we asked the Lord to deliver us, we believed that He answered our petition, for God cannot lie.

9. Put every area of your life under the lordship of Jesus.

> I beseech you therefore, brethren, by the mercies of God, that you present your bodies a living sacrifice, holy, acceptable to God, which is your reasonable service. And do not be conformed to this world, but be transformed by the renewing of your mind, that you may prove what is that good and acceptable and perfect will of God.
>
> —ROMANS 12:1–2

Present your bodies a living sacrifice, holy and acceptable unto God. The Greek word for "holy" in this passage is *hagios*, and it means, "sacred, physically pure, morally blameless or religious, consecrated, most holy one or thing, and saint." God, through Paul, said this is our reasonable service. If we fail in this area, we give entrance

155

to Satan. Satan cannot legally afflict a saint. Sin, however, opens the door to him when we are out of fellowship with the Lord. Paul goes on to say, "Don't conform to the world, be transformed, and renew your mind."

The world settles for second best because they don't know the best. We are admonished to seek what is the highest standard of living as our reasonable service to God. James 4:7 exhorts us, "Submit yourselves therefore to God. Resist the devil, and he will flee from you" (KJV).

I know this scripture is being used a lot, but it is at the very heart of the matter of deliverance. Our deliverance or escape is through God. He will do it as we obey, believe, submit, trust, and have faith in Him.

> Being confident of this very thing, that He who has begun a good work in you will complete it until the day of Jesus Christ.
> —PHILIPPIANS 1:6

Thank You, Lord!

10. Get rid of unforgiveness, resentment, and bitterness toward everyone.

> And whenever you stand praying, if you have anything against anyone, forgive him, that your Father in heaven may also forgive you your trespasses. But if you do not forgive, neither will your Father in heaven forgive your trespasses.
> —MARK 11:25–26

Prayer is a major factor in maintaining deliverance. You need to commune with the Lord on a daily basis. A major part of your prayer life is to seek forgiveness of sins you might commit in your daily walk. John wrote, "If we confess our sins, He is faithful and just to forgive us our sins and cleanse us from all unrighteousness" (1 John 1:9).

If you want to be forgiven, you must also forgive. Sometimes that trespass against us is a blatant assault such as gossip, backbiting, verbal abuse, and so forth. However, sometimes we may also have to forgive the driver who cuts us off or the waitress who snubbed us. It is very easy to hold anger against people at times. We must be careful.

> If I regard iniquity in my heart, the Lord will not hear me.
>
> —PSALM 66:18, KJV

The word *iniquity* covers a lot of mischief we can hide or keep in our heart, especially if we have not forgiven someone. Many times we hear the statement, "I have forgiven him or her, but I'll never forget what they have done to me."

Has this person really forgiven the offense? Or is he still holding on to it, allowing it to fester in his heart? If we are harboring an offense, we will tend to get very bitter toward the person. When bitterness sets in, we are in trouble. Paul said to Simon the magician in Acts 8:23,

"For I see that you are poisoned by bitterness and bound by iniquity." God considers bitterness a poison.

11. Submit to God's authority. Wives, submit to your husbands; husbands, love your wives.

> Wives, submit to your own husbands, as to the Lord. For the husband is head of the wife, as also Christ is head of the church; and He is the Savior of the body. Therefore, just as the church is subject to Christ, so let the wives be to their own husbands in everything. Husbands, love your wives, just as Christ also loved the church and gave Himself for her.
>
> —EPHESIANS 5:22–25

Again, don't allow Satan any door of entry. We have specific commands from the Lord. If we obey, the devil cannot penetrate our armor, and he must flee from us.

> Let every soul be subject to the governing authorities. For there is no authority except from God, and the authorities that exist are appointed by God. Therefore whoever resists the authority resists the ordinance of God, and those who resist will bring judgment on themselves.
>
> —ROMANS 13:1–2

God has placed you under authority to His Word for your own good. Sometimes it feels like you must follow a lot of rules, but God is only looking out for your well-being. Being under authority helps you to maintain a clear conscience.

12. Do not turn your back on your salvation.

In Judges 10:6–14 the children of Israel clearly turned away from their salvation and God's deliverance to worship other gods. God was very angry with them. It is a dangerous thing to get into this position with God. He said in verse 13, "Yet you have forsaken Me and served other gods. Therefore I will deliver you no more."

God's people were delivered from their slavery, and God saved them from their persecutors. However, their demonic oppressions returned. They were healed, yet they continued oppressed. Why? Because they refused to walk in obedience to God's laws and once again fell into sin. Sin again produced death.

We cannot expect to continue receiving God's blessings and expect to keep our healing or deliverance or any other blessing, whether physical or spiritual, if we refuse to walk in our salvation and obedience.

> Afterward Jesus found him in the temple, and said to him, "See, you have been made well. Sin no more, lest a worse thing come upon you."
> —JOHN 5:14

For those who would say the previous scripture from Judges is Old Testament and that we have a new covenant, Jesus is saying the same thing in John 5:14. If you continue to sin after your deliverance or healing, something worse may come upon you. The lame man in Bethesda was responsible for maintaining his own healing by doing and obeying God's laws. Jesus warned him that if he continued sinning, something worse would come upon him.

In any deliverance it is the responsibility of the person delivered to maintain his walk with the Lord in order to remain free. The Lord does His part by delivering us; now we must do our part by walking faithfully in our salvation and our freedom and not turning back.

One of the attributes lacking today among believers is integrity. Many Christians are indifferent to sin. They believe that they can continue sinning after they have been saved. Many times this is the cause of some distorted view or teaching about the grace of God. There is a way to lose our salvation—by the choices we make.

> For if, after they have escaped the pollutions of the world through the knowledge of the Lord and Savior Jesus Christ, they are again entangled in them and overcome, the latter end is worse for them than the beginning.
> —2 PETER 2:20

This scripture does not need a lot of comment. I believe God is exhorting us to take His Word seriously. He is telling us not to return to Egypt after we have been delivered out of bondage.

Do not return to worldly lusts and desires after you

have been delivered out of demonic oppression. Do not turn your back on His saving grace.

> Salvation is a continuous working of God in us, and He needs our cooperation.

We can achieve this by doing what the following scripture teaches:

> Therefore we also, since we are surrounded by so great a cloud of witnesses, let us lay aside every weight, and the sin which so easily ensnares us, and let us run with endurance the race that is set before us, looking unto Jesus, the author and finisher of our faith, who for the joy that was set before Him endured the cross, despising the shame, and has sat down at the right hand of the throne of God.
> —HEBREWS 12:1–2

We meet many agonized Christians in our meetings who come to the altar to repent of ensnaring sins. Their urgent cry is to know whether God will have mercy and receive them again after they trespassed and turned their back on God and wandered in the wilderness. Their testimony is usually similar—"Where was God when I needed him?" "Why didn't He answer my prayers?" "I just got tired and fed up, and I made a decision to just walk away and ignore God just as He had ignored me."

When a believer trespasses, he is entering somebody

else's land unlawfully. He is intruding and he is sinning. But once a believer confesses, repents, and receives prayer, he is forgiven and also receives healing and wholeness. Praise God! No matter how many times a child of God falls and fails, God is willing to forgive and restore him.

> Confess your trespasses to one another, and pray for one another, that you may be healed. The effective, fervent prayer of a righteous man avails much.
>
> —JAMES 5:16

A believer must be very careful to understand that God does not tolerate other gods before Him (Exod. 20:3). Getting angry, sulking, and ignoring God is not the same as forsaking almighty God for other gods. When a person forsakes God after tasting and knowing Him and His Word, after experiencing His power and His presence, and he opens his heart to render worship and adoration to another entity or god, he's in danger of losing his salvation. But if the person truly repents and forsakes all other gods, God will have mercy and forgive and restore.

As we obey and cooperate with the Lord, we have the following promise:

> Now it shall come to pass, if you diligently obey the voice of the LORD your God, to observe carefully all His commandments which I command you today, that the LORD your God will set you

high above all nations of the earth. And all these
blessings shall come upon you and overtake you,
because you obey the voice of the LORD your
God.

—DEUTERONOMY 28:1–2

REVIEW—HOW TO KEEP YOUR DELIVERANCE

1. *Do not discuss* your deliverance with
anyone who does not believe in this
ministry (Matt. 7:6; Mark 6:5–6).

2. *Destroy* all occult objects and literature.
Be careful what you bring into your home.
Read only those things pleasing to God
(Deut. 18:9–13; Acts 19:18–19).

3. *Study* the scriptures daily and spend time
apart with God (Ps. 119:105; Matt. 4:4; Acts
17:11; Eph. 4:12; 2 Tim. 2:15; James 1:22–25;
1 Pet. 2:2).

4. *Develop* a consistent prayer life. Pray in the
spirit many times daily (1 Cor. 14:14–15; 1
Thess. 5:17; James 5:16; Jude 20).

5. *Have spiritual fellowship* with other members of the body of Christ, particularly a
group where the gifts of the Spirit are manifested (1 Cor. 12:7–14; Heb. 10:25).

6. *Guard* your mind and thoughts. Refuse to think negative, critical, resentful or selfish thoughts (Prov. 6:12; Phil. 4:8).

7. *Use the authority* given to you in the name of Jesus to bind, rebuke, and cast out anything that is of the devil (Mark 16:17; Eph. 1:5–6).

8. *Confess* your deliverance by faith, not feelings (Joel 2:32; 2 Cor. 5:7; Heb. 10:38; 11:6; 1 John 5:14–15).

9. *Put every area* of your life under the lordship of Jesus Christ (Rom. 12:1–2; James 4:7).

10. *Get rid* of unforgiveness, resentment, and bitterness toward anyone affecting you (Ps. 66:18; Mark 11:25–26).

11. *Submit* to your spouse and to spiritual authority (Rom. 13:1–2; Eph. 5:22–25).

12. *Do not turn back* from your salvation (Heb. 6:4–6; 2 Pet. 2:20).

There is therefore now no condemnation to those who are in Christ Jesus, who do not walk according to the flesh, but according to the Spirit.
—ROMANS 8:1

Amen!

Living in Freedom From the Enemy's Attacks

THE WILL OF GOD FOR YOUR LIFE

*The world and its desires pass away, but the
man who does the will of God lives forever.*

—1 JOHN 2:17, NIV

THE WORD OF God says that we must know what
God's will is for our lives. Paul tells us, "Therefore
do not be unwise, but understand what the will
of the Lord is" (Eph. 5:17). Yet so many Christians ask,
"How do I know God's will for my life?"

It is a great blessing to know God's will for our lives.
God imparts to us divine guidance day by day and the
wisdom we need to make important decisions.

Christians without the experience and the power of
the Holy Spirit in their lives spend much of their time
out of the will of God. Fear and frustrations hinder their
spiritual growth because of doubt and unbelief. They feel
unfulfilled with no purpose in their lives.

It is God's will for every Christian to receive the

promise of the Father—to be filled with the Holy Spirit. Then we will understand what the will of the Lord is for us in every area of our life. *God's most important will for every born-again believer is that we learn to yield completely to His Spirit.*

The Holy Spirit in the believer produces *boldness* to speak, pray, and teach the Word.

> And when they had prayed, the place where they were assembled together was shaken; and they were all filled with the Holy Spirit, and they spoke the word of God with boldness.
>
> —ACTS 4:31

The Holy Spirit in the believer produces joy.

> And the disciples were filled with joy and with the Holy Spirit.
>
> —ACTS 13:52

The Holy Spirit in the believer produces knowledge of His will, wisdom, and spiritual understanding.

> For this reason we also, since the day we heard it, do not cease to pray for you, and to ask that you may be filled with the knowledge of His will in all wisdom and spiritual understanding.
>
> —COLOSSIANS 1:9

The Holy Spirit in the believer is able to prophesy.

Now his father Zacharias was filled with the
Holy Spirit, and prophesied.

—LUKE 1:67

To know the will of God, we must be crucified with
Christ. It is a spiritual position. It is a walk of faith. It
is believing in an invisible God who created heaven and
earth. It is a matter of total trust.

> I have been crucified with Christ; it is no longer
> I who live, but Christ lives in me; and the life
> which I now live in the flesh I live by faith in
> the Son of God, who loved me and gave Himself
> for me.
>
> —GALATIANS 2:20

Today more than ever we need the power of the Holy
Spirit to direct our steps and to help us understand the
times we are living in. In our travels we are seeing people
of all walks of life and denominations come to Christ
and be filled with the Holy Spirit.

*The baptism of the Holy Spirit is the doorway to a
deeper experience with God.* It is an invitation to become
one with Christ. It is a higher calling into the blessed life.

God is calling His people to a more intimate relationship with Him, allowing the Holy Spirit to teach us the
meaning of a life crucified and sold out to Christ.

By our appropriation of Galatians 2:20, the resurrection power of Jesus Christ may be manifested through

us. Only then will we spiritually become grown men and women able to obtain God's higher purpose for our lives.

God's will for every believer is to understand the purpose for which he has been filled with His Spirit and to learn how to submit and be guided by the Spirit. If more Christians understood that they have not been called by God *to be anything* or *do anything* for Him, *but to submit completely to the guidance and direction of the Holy Spirit* and to bear the fruit of the Spirit, God's people today would be enjoying a different position of authority, dominion, and abundance.

Jesus said:

> You are My friends if you do whatever I command you. No longer do I call you servants, for a servant does not know what his master is doing; but I have called you friends, for all things that I heard from My Father I have made known to you. You did not choose Me, but I chose you and appointed you that you should go and bear fruit, and that your fruit should remain, that whatever you ask the Father in My name He may give you.
> —JOHN 15:14–16

This teaching about surrendering, crucifying the flesh, and dying to self is not very popular. We all like the part about producing much grain and enjoying a harvest of blessings. Millions of Christians are *just getting by*, barely making ends meet. Their substance can be weighed and measured from hand to mouth. No treasures stored up.

No savings in the bank and no relief from the attacks of the enemy.

> Most assuredly, I say to you, unless a grain of wheat falls into the ground and dies, it remains alone; but if it dies, it produces much grain.
> —JOHN 12:24

The walk of the surrendered life is not trying to *do* more for God after receiving the Holy Spirit.

...not praying more

...not reading the Bible more

...not witnessing more

...not increasing our religious efforts

...not our good works

God's will for us is a total surrender to the leading of the Holy Spirit in our lives. It is not Christ *and* you but Christ *in* you that will make your life effective and that will produce much fruit.

To accept this sold-out life is to understand that being filled with the Spirit is not God's call to work for Him but to learn to move with Him.

To live an overcomer's life, you must go beyond the blessings into the power stream of God. You must learn to move only at the leading of the Spirit and under His direction.

God is preparing an end-time army of fearless believers who will be so sensitive to the voice of the Spirit that they will immediately respond to His leading without questions or doubt.

A soldier is not called to work for the army, but he is to work and move under command. He learns to deny self and submit to authority.

There are people who will ask us, "How do you know you're doing God's will?" Simple—we're at peace. The name of the state, the address we live in, or the kind of work we are doing does not matter. As long as we are at peace with God, accountable and submitted to each other, and a good loving example to our children, we are in God's will. We submit to God and His Word.

God did not call you merely to do good works. Every Christian is capable of this. His will for you is that you should become fruitful in every good work and that you love others as He loves you.

Living the dedicated, abundant, and victorious life is impossible without total faith in God. You must put your total trust in God. The life of faith simply means to trust and obey the Lord with all your heart. God is faithful to His Word. This is God's will for you. All other things flow from this position.

> Let us hold fast the confession of our hope without wavering, for He who promised is faithful.
>
> —Hebrews 10:23

THE PURPOSE OF LIFE

We were all created by God to live a fulfilling and fruitful life. One of the great tragedies of our time is the growing aimlessness and lack of purpose in the lives of people today. Most people have no idea what life is all about and only live according to what others say.

By studying the Word carefully, we can see that God intended for man to:

- Walk in relationship with Him

- Walk in relationship with one another

- Take dominion and authority over the earth and rule over it

Instead, man's disobedience allowed temptation to overcome him, separating him from God's will and purpose for his life.

In order to walk in relationship with God, repentance is necessary. A literal change of direction must take place in the heart. A complete trust and faith in God must take place. Prayer must become the means of communication between man and God. If we are to grow and mature, confession and declaration of God's Word must become a lifestyle.

DANGERS OF UNBELIEF

Many Christians are spiritually crippled because every time the Holy Spirit moves in their lives, they immediately try to analyze God's instructions. The mind is like a filter. When the minds of immature believers receive the instructions of God, before acting on the instructions God has given, those minds often produce doubt and unbelief. We are convinced that if there was no devil to oppose the saints, they would still have problems walking in the Spirit because of their reasoning minds.

There is a key that will unlock the wonderful works of God in your life if you will just use it. That key is to act in obedience when God speaks *before* you give your mind the opportunity to reason away what He said.

Be daring in your walk with God, willing to take a risk by using your authority in Christ Jesus. Peter developed a reckless attitude when it came to obeying God's voice. He knew something good always happened when Jesus was on the scene.

God hates unbelief. Unbelief comes when you stop to analyze what God has said. When you analyze, your mind becomes paralyzed. Many of God's people are spiritually paralyzed because they have never literally accepted the Word of the Lord. Every time God speaks through His Word, rather than accepting and acting upon it at once, it is processed through their intellectual filter and then rejected or accepted.

You may wonder why many new believers receive an

instant healing or answer to prayer. It is because they do not try to analyze God's Word; they simply accept what it says.

> He sent His Word and healed them,
> And delivered them from their destructions.
>
> —PSALM 107:20

13

How to Recognize True and False Doctrines

The day of your watchmen has come, the day God visits you. Now is the time of their confusion.

—Micah 7:4, NIV

WE ARE LIVING in the last days—*days of confusion.* These are the prophetic days in which it is difficult to distinguish the good and the bad, what is real and what is not, the legitimate and the things that are fantasy. However, our God has anticipated these times, and He has left us specific instructions to guide us in the days of tribulation. God has established a covenant with His people. If we pay attention to the Word, we will be able to discern truth from false teachings.

The following are some biblical guidelines to distinguish between true and false doctrines.

1. Any doctrine that places the Bible on the same level as all other common books is false. The Bible, the Word of God, is above all and superior to all other written works.

I will praise You with my whole heart…
For You have magnified Your word above all
Your name.
—PSALM 138:1–2

The Bible is above all the opinions or wisdom of men; it is above whatever the mind may say or opinionate. It supersedes all the intelligence of the wise, the geniuses, all politicians, and is above all.

2. Any doctrine that puts the Bible under a question of doubt, whether in totality or in part, is taking the risk of removing its virtue from those who are not firm in their faith and understanding of the true divine inspiration of the sacred Scriptures. The Bible is divinely inspired without defects or errors. It is the divine revelation given by inspiration of God.

The law of the LORD is perfect, converting the
soul;
The testimony of the LORD is sure, making wise
the simple.
—PSALM 19:7

Oh, the depth of the riches both of the wisdom and knowledge of God! How unsearchable are His judgments and His ways past finding out!

—ROMANS 11:33

All Scripture is given by inspiration of God, and is profitable for doctrine, for reproof, for correction, for instruction in righteousness, that the man of God may be complete, thoroughly equipped for every good work.

—2 TIMOTHY 3:16–17

3. The doctrines that try to accommodate the passages of the Bible to permit their abominable sins and try to combine the biblical and sanctified teachings with the times, trends, and different movements are false doctrines. Any doctrine that tries to change the significance of Scripture by removing its virtue as questionable is a false doctrine. God does not change. He is unchangeable. He is the same yesterday, today, and forever. God's Word, His commandments, and His promises are unchangeable, immutable, eternal, and infallible.

For I am the LORD, I do not change.

—MALACHI 3:6

> I tell you the truth, until heaven and earth disappear, not the smallest letter, not the least stroke of a pen, will by any means disappear from the Law until everything is accomplished.
>
> —MATTHEW 5:18, NIV

> Jesus Christ is the same yesterday, today, and forever.
>
> —HEBREWS 13:8

4. When doctrines deny the basic and infallible teachings of the sacred Scriptures, such as the existence of heaven, hell, the Trinity, and such, and instead substitute their own logical and human rationality, they are false.

5. Any doctrine that sets the Bible as a historical book and of little importance, causing people to lose their interest in it and to see all things as in the past and not for today, is a false doctrine. The plan of God is to elevate His Word and confirm it in all times (Jer. 1:12) and to show the world that the Bible is true and real, is the fount of all wisdom, and is powerful today (Ps. 119:97–104; 1 Cor. 2:1–5).

And they went out and preached everywhere, the Lord working with them and confirming the word through the accompanying signs.

—MARK 16:20

For the word of God is living and powerful, and sharper than any two-edged sword, piercing even to the division of soul and spirit, and of joints and marrow, and is a discerner of the thoughts and intents of the heart.

—HEBREWS 4:12

6. All doctrines that try to put veils on the sacred Scriptures and try to impede the people who read it, hiding behind such thoughts as "It is only for the wise and not all can or should read it," are false and erroneous. In many cases the propagators of these doctrines change certain words or certain passages by adding explanations or personal opinions. They take advantage of many people and guide them to accept things as they believe or opinionate. But they do not realize that they prevent the free will given by God to man to choose and decide for themselves their final destination according to what God teaches in His Holy Word.

> Blessed is he who reads and those who hear the
> words of this prophecy, and keep those things
> which are written in it; for the time is near.
> —Revelation 1:3; see also John 5:39

7. Any doctrine that tries to mix or complete
   the Word of God with human opinions or
   other books, giving them the same value
   and authority as the Bible, is false. Only
   the Bible is divinely inspired. It is true that
   there are many other books that help us to
   understand with more clarity some difficult
   passages, but none of these are divinely
   inspired or could replace the Word of God.
   We believe that the only foundation of
   divine inspiration is the sacred Scriptures,
   and they are unique in their totality.

Notes on False Doctrines

Any doctrine or teaching that denies or in any manner
causes doubt or unbelief concerning all the things taught
in the Scriptures is inspired by demons.

Any religion that denies the inspiration of the Bible
or the reality of God as a person or that denies Christ as
the divine Son of God, His preexistence, His virgin birth,
His divinity, His miraculous and mysterious supernatural power, His burial, His resurrection, and corporal
manifestation after His resurrection, His ascension, or

His second coming to establish His kingdom forever is of Satan's origin.

Any doctrine that denies the Christian experience— such as the new birth; the cleansing of sin; living free from sin; divine health; the baptism of the Holy Spirit; the gifts of the Spirit; miracles and signs that follow those who believe; answers to prayer; the fulfilling of the promises for health, happiness, prosperity, and many other Christian experiences of the New Testament; Satan; demons; sickness; sin; the fall of man; the creation of everything by God; and man as a mortal being—is a false doctrine.

RULES TO RECOGNIZE

True, sound doctrine will elevate the Word of God above all.

It will always give it a preeminent place. The Word of God is the fountain of living water that cleanses, restores, and transforms mankind.

> Sanctify them by Your truth. Your word is truth.
> —JOHN 17:17; SEE ALSO 2 TIMOTHY 3:16

The Bible is precise and full of wisdom.

It reveals to all men the dangers of living apart from God and the perils of hell. The Word of God extends an invitation to man to repent and to partake of eternal life. It reveals clearly the unity and perfection of one God in three distinct persons—Father, Son, and Holy Spirit.

Hell exists and is a place prepared for the final judgment of Satan and his angels.

It is also a place for all those who, after hearing of the love of God and the provision He made for the forgiveness of all their sins, harden themselves and never repent. For this reason they will be cast into hell forever.

> Serpents, brood of vipers! How can you escape the condemnation of hell?
>
> —MATTHEW 23:33

> But I will show you whom you should fear: Fear Him who, after He has killed, has power to cast into hell; yes, I say to you, fear Him!
>
> —LUKE 12:5; SEE ALSO MATTHEW 10:28; 18:9

> So it was that the beggar died, and was carried by the angels to Abraham's bosom. The rich man also died and was buried. And being in torments in Hades, he lifted up his eyes and saw Abraham afar off, and Lazarus in his bosom.
>
> —LUKE 16:22–23

The Bible teaches us that hell is real and that it exists. The Bible also speaks of heaven as a place of peace and tranquility, where there will be no crying or pain and where Christ will dwell and wipe away all tears from your eyes.

But I say to you, do not swear at all: neither by heaven, for it is God's throne.

—MATTHEW 5:34

Our Father in heaven,
Hallowed be Your name.
Your kingdom come.
Your will be done
On earth as it is in heaven.

—MATTHEW 6:9–10

But lay up for yourselves treasures in heaven, where neither moth nor rust destroys.

—MATTHEW 6:20

The Bible presents to us the existence of only one supreme God in three distinct persons.

Any doctrine that teaches the contrary or puts doubt in these truths is of the devil.

The grace of the Lord Jesus Christ, and the love of God, and the communion of the Holy Spirit be with you all. Amen.

—2 CORINTHIANS 13:14

For there are three that bear witness in heaven: the Father, the Word [Christ, John 1:1], and the Holy Spirit; and these three are one.

—1 JOHN 5:7

Sound doctrine allows man to affirm in his heart all the promises of God.

We can take them seriously, believing and profiting from them (Ps. 119:9–10).

> And that from childhood you have known the Holy Scriptures, which are able to make you wise for salvation through faith which is in Christ Jesus.
>
> —2 TIMOTHY 3:15

Sound doctrine guides the believer to have an effective and dynamic faith in God.

It teaches us to believe in its potential, its power, and its perfection. God's sound doctrines will give us good judgment and a clear understanding about all the evil and error in the world.

> For whatever things were written before were written for our learning, that we through the patience and comfort of the Scriptures might have hope.
>
> —ROMANS 15:4

Sound doctrine is founded upon the eternal promises of God.

All the teachings of sound doctrine will lead a person to a clear understanding of righteousness. It teaches the believer to triumph over all evil and to use good judgment. It teaches believers how to overcome adversity through absolute faith in Jesus Christ.

I can do all things through Christ who strengthens me.

—PHILIPPIANS 4:13

For the grace of God that brings salvation has appeared to all men, teaching us that, denying ungodliness and worldly lusts, we should live soberly, righteously, and godly in the present age.

—TITUS 2:11–12

Sound doctrine places Jesus Christ as Lord of lords and as the Savior of all mankind.

As the only mediator between God and man, He is the same always, yesterday, today, and forever (1 Tim. 2:5; Heb. 13:8). Christ is the only one who can save. He invites us to confess our sins to Him with confidence because He has the power to forgive us, restore us, cleanse us, and sanctify us, and He has given us authority to reign with Him forever (1 Cor. 6:9–11; Heb. 4:15–16).

Christ does not accuse or despise us. He directs us and helps us to conquer all bondage of the enemy, such as bad habits, curses, evil spirits, disturbances, and sin.

Come to Me, all you who labor and are heavy laden, and I will give you rest.

—MATTHEW 11:28

All that the Father gives Me will come to Me, and the one who comes to Me I will by no means cast out.

—JOHN 6:37

Then Jesus spoke to them again, saying, "I am the light of the world. He who follows Me shall not walk in darkness, but have the light of life."

—JOHN 8:12; SEE ALSO JOHN 14:6

Sound doctrine allows the believer to understand the greatness and depth of God's love.

God's love toward man is seen through the thousands of promises in His Word. It helps us understand and love the Word of God in a deeper way, guiding us to make wise decisions that build our faith and our relationship with the Holy Spirit.

Only be strong and very courageous, that you may observe to do according to all the law which Moses My servant commanded you; do not turn from it to the right hand or to the left, that you may prosper wherever you go. This Book of the Law shall not depart from your mouth, but you shall meditate in it day and night, that you may observe to do according to all that is written in it. For then you will make your way prosperous, and then you will have good success.

—JOSHUA 1:7–8

POWERFUL DECLARATIONS THAT COUNTERACT THE ATTACKS OF THE ENEMY

When Satan brings doubt

The Word declares that if I speak to my mountain of problems and command it to go in the name of Jesus, it must obey me if I believe without doubting in my heart. I believe I have what I am asking for in faith [Mark 11:23]!

When Satan brings insomnia

Father, Your Word declares that if I keep Your Word before my eyes and in my heart, it will be life and healing to me. When I lie down to sleep, I will not be afraid, and my sleep will be sweet. I believe this, and I command insomnia to let go its hold on me, in Jesus's name [Prov. 3:21–24; Isa. 57:2].

When there is danger and fear

Father, I believe Your angels encamp around and about me to defend me. I will not fear or be afraid. You have given me authority over all the power of the enemy. In Jesus's name I command fear to go now and God's peace to guard my heart [Ps. 34:7; Luke 10:19].

When there is laziness

Father, please give me the strength to recover my vitality and my energy. I renounce the works of the enemy in my life, and I loose myself from all curses and iniquities from my family and my ancestors. I declare that I'm free from the curse of laziness in the name of Jesus, amen [Prov. 6:6–11].

When there is apparent defeat

Lord, I stand on Your Word believing that what the enemy has meant for defeat, You are able to turn into a victory. You cause me to triumph and have victory through Christ Jesus. Thank You for sustaining me during this time. In Jesus's name, amen [Isa. 59:19; Rom. 8:37; 1 Cor. 15:57].

When there is lack

Father, I repent of all the things I have or have not done that have caused lack and want to affect my life. I set myself free from this curse and ask for wisdom and understanding to trust You with my substance. Teach me, Holy Spirit, to be a good steward and to obey God's Word. My God is able to supply all my needs [Phil. 4:19].

When there is worry and anxiety

Father, You have promised to guard my heart and to preserve me with Your peace. I command all worry and anxiety out of my heart and thoughts in the name of Jesus. I trust You, my Lord. You have not given me a spirit of fear. You have given me power and authority and a sound mind. Thank You for this promise, in Jesus's name [Isa. 26:3; Phil. 4:6–7; 2 Tim. 1:7].

When there is opposition against you.

Father, Your Word declares that no weapon formed against me shall prosper, and everyone who talks lies about me, You will condemn. I thank You for this heritage [Isa. 41:11; 54:17; 2 Cor. 10:4–6].

When there is sickness

Father, Your Word declares that You heal all my diseases, and You redeem my life from destruction. You were wounded and bruised, and by Your stripes I am healed. I thank You for such a great sacrifice, and I believe that I am healed in the name of Jesus [Ps. 103:1–5; Isa. 53:4–5; Matt. 8:17; Luke 13:11–13].

When there is lack of faith

My Lord, please forgive my incredulity. Help me to remain steadfast believing Your Word. For we walk by faith and not by sight. From this day forward I make a decision to walk by faith. Thank You, Holy Spirit, for Your help while I learn to live by faith. In Jesus's name, amen [Matt. 14:31; Rom. 10:17; Gal. 5:5].

When we need love

Father, thank You for Your gift of love because even when we were sinners, Christ shed His blood for us. Thank You for Your amazing love that has been poured in our hearts and continues to sustain me [Rom. 5:5–9].

When we feel hatred

Lord, forgive me for feeling such deep feelings of hatred when someone offends me. I repent of this offense, and I pray that You have mercy toward my enemies. Your Word declares that hatred stirs up strife, but love covers all sins. Thank You for opening my spiritual understanding to know that I have authority over the spirit of hatred and must not allow it to rule over me [Prov. 10:12].

When there is weariness and discouragement

Father, thank You that Your Word declares You give power to the weak, and to those who have no might You increase their strength. When I am weary, You cause me to mount up with wings as an eagle. I declare that discouragement shall not have dominion over me [Isa. 40:28–31; Heb. 12:3].

When there is gluttony and lack of self-control

Father, I repent of this habit of gluttony. Your Word declares that a person who lacks self-control is like a person whose walls are broken down. Thank You for helping me create healthy habits that will bring glory and honor

to Your name and help me feel and look better
[Prov. 23:2; 25:28; Rom. 14:17].

When there are suicidal tendencies

Father, You formed me in my mother's womb
with purpose and destiny. The thief comes to
steal, kill, and destroy, but You come to give
life in abundance. Thank You for redeeming
me of all my sins. I declare that I belong to
You and no weapon formed against me shall
prosper. In the name of Jesus, I bind the spirit
of suicide and cast it out of my life. I loose
the peace and the love of God into my heart.
Amen [Isa. 54:17; John 10:10].

Against the love of money

Father, help me remain aware that it is You
who provide all my needs and not my own
strength or abilities. Help me to be satisfied
and not tempted by the love of money. Your
Word declares that those who seek the Lord
shall not lack any good thing [Ps. 34:10; Hag.
2:8; 1 Tim. 6:8–10].

When hope is lost

Lord, thank You for filling me with hope, joy,
and peace so that I may abound in hope

*by the power of the Holy Spirit [Rom. 15:13;
1 Thess. 4:13–16].*

When there are carnal desires

*Father, I thank You for the Holy Spirit helping
me overcome all the desires of my flesh. I set
myself free from all learned habits that are
not pleasing to You. In Jesus's name, I bring
all evil thoughts that invade my mind, captive
to the obedience of Christ [2 Cor. 10:5; Gal.
5:19–21; Eph. 5:3–10].*

When there is pride

*Lord, keep my heart from being lifted up and
my eyes from being lofty and arrogant [Isa.
2:11; 16:6–12; Ezek. 28:17].*

When there is vanity

*Father, turn away my eyes from looking at
worthless things, and revive me in Your way
[Ps. 119:37; Eccles. 1:4, 17].*

Against the old man (sin nature)

*Lord Jesus, thank You for the new nature that
You have given me. I am not the same. Thank
You for filling my life with Your mercy, kind-
ness, humility, meekness, and longsuffering.*

Help me not to desire the things of the past. I submit to Your lordship. In the name of Jesus, amen [Rom. 6:6; Eph. 4:22–32; Col. 3:1–14].

Against lukewarmness

Help me, Father, to remain steadfast and to be found faithful by You, not lukewarm but sold out to the kingdom of God [1 Cor. 4:2; Rev. 3:16].

Against filthy thoughts

Help me, Holy Spirit, to guard my thoughts. For out of the heart proceed evil thoughts, murders, adulteries, fornications, thefts, false witness, and blasphemies. These are the things that defile a man [Matt. 15:19–20].

Against discouragement and anguish

Father, during this time of discouragement and anguish in my life, help me not to lose heart. For my soul trusts in You, and in the shadow of Your wings I will make my refuge until these calamities have passed by [1 Sam. 30:6; Ps. 57:1; Luke 18:1].

Against corruption

Father, I thank You because You will not abandon me to the realm of the dead, nor will You let Your faithful one see decay [Ps. 16:10, NIV].

Against death

Thank You, Father, for death is swallowed up in victory through our Lord Jesus Christ. We have this great promise that whoever believes in Him shall not perish but have eternal life [John 3:15; 1 Cor. 15:56–58; Rev. 1:18; 20:14].

Against lies

Lord, protect my mind from believing the lies of the enemy. Your Word declares that no weapon formed against me shall prosper, and every tongue that rises against me in judgment You shall condemn [1 Kings 22:19–23; Isa. 54:17; Rev. 21:8; 22:15].

Against attitudes of envy, criticism, impatience

My Lord, guard my heart from allowing yokes of wrong attitudes to invade my life, causing Your blessing to depart from me and hindering healing from springing forth speedily. Let patience have its perfect work, that I may be perfect and complete, lacking nothing [Isa. 58:8-9; Gal. 5:19-21; Eph. 4:31; Col. 3:5-8; James 1:3-4].

Against witchcraft and its works

Father God, if there is anything adverse in my life caused by witchcraft and the occult, whether in my past or through my ancestors, I repent of it right now and ask for Your forgiveness of all sins and iniquities. I bind all demonic spirits that may be involved, commanding them out of my life and my family. I loose the healing power of God and complete restoration of all things the enemy has stolen from me, in the name of Jesus, amen [Exod. 22:18; Lev. 19:31; 20:6; Deut. 18:10-12; Nah. 3:4].

Against false prophecy

Holy Spirit, I ask for wisdom and understanding to know the difference between false prophesy and true prophesy from the Spirit of God. I will test the spirits, whether they are of God, because many false prophets have gone out into the world. Every spirit that confesses that Jesus Christ has come in the flesh is of God, and every spirit that does not confess that Jesus Christ has come in the flesh is not of God. Reveal the spirit of the Antichrist, which you have heard was coming, and is now already in the world [Matt. 7:15-23; 1 John 4:1-6; Rev. 16:13, 19-20].

Against the devil himself

Thank You, Father, because Jesus defeated the devil on the cross of Calvary. The devil has no part or portion in our life. The Lord is faithful to guard us from the evil one. The devil was cast out of heaven, and You will establish me and guard me from the evil one [Gen. 3:15; Isa. 27:1; 2 Thess. 3:3; Rev. 12:7-9].

Against idolatry

Lord, Your commandment to Your children is very clear: "Thou shalt have no other gods before me. Thou shalt not make unto thee any graven image, or any likeness of any thing that is in heaven above, or that is in the earth beneath, or that is in the water under the earth: Thou shalt not bow down thyself to them, nor serve them: for I the Lord thy God am a jealous God, visiting the iniquity of the fathers upon the children unto the third and fourth generation of them that hate me." Father, forgive us if we have trespassed this commandment. Holy Spirit, help us to discern all the things that may be considered idols and that rob us of our time and love for God [Exod. 20:3–5, KJV; 1 Cor. 10:19–20; Rev. 9:20].

Against the spirit of error

Father, Your Spirit clearly says that in latter times some will abandon the faith and follow deceiving spirits and things taught by demons. Such teachings come through hypocritical liars, whose consciences have been seared as with a hot iron. Help us to discern the spirit of error and the spirit of truth [1 Tim. 4:1–2].

Against secret covenants with death or the devil

Father, if there has ever been any secret covenants made with death or the devil against my person or my bloodline, I plead the blood of Jesus and break and annul all covenants made against us, whether in ignorance or knowingly. In Jesus's name I declare freedom from all curses. Amen [Isa. 28:17–18].

Against sorrow

Thank You, my Lord, because You are my strength and my fortress. You turn my sorrow into joy. You heal my broken spirit. I will not sorrow, for the joy of the Lord is my strength. I will develop a merry heart, which is like medicine [Neh. 8:10; Prov. 17:22].

ABOUT THE AUTHORS

Drs. JOHN AND Iris Delgado have been involved in the teaching of the Word and Christian counseling for more than thirty-five years. They are the founders of Vision International Leadership Network and Crowned With Purpose. They have the confidence that now more than ever is the time for believers to seize the moment and exercise their authority in Christ Jesus.

Both John and Iris teach and minister about deliverance and the importance of helping people who are depressed and anguished to come out of spiritual prisons. They conduct seminars and special meetings in the United States and abroad.

Dr. John Delgado is the president of Vision International University of Florida, with outreaches in the United States and abroad—a ministry equipping Christian leaders for the work of the kingdom all around the world.

They earned their doctor of ministry and Christian counseling degrees from Vision International University in California.

As authors, Iris Delgado has written the following books in English and in Spanish:

Satan, You Can't Have My Children

Satan, You Can't Have My Marriage

Satan, You Can't Have My Miracle

Satan, You Can't Have My Promises

Dr. John Delgado has written:

Prayer Training Manual

Men of Impact in Times of Crisis

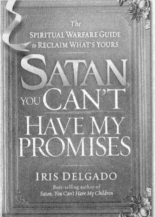
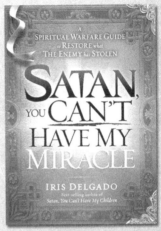
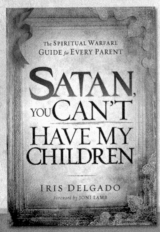
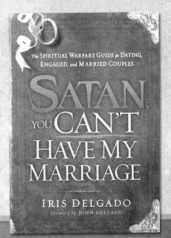